"Duffett is on a quintessential quest for communicating the Bible in a powerful and persuasive manner. While the author is widely read and sociologically astute, the book's primary value is the fine blend of hermeneutics and homiletics with a commitment to touch the biblically disenchanted. It enables one to move from the text to the sermon to the world."

—*Warren S. Benson, Ph.D.*
Trinity Evangelical Divinity School

"Every great message needs to be translated—sometimes into a different language, always into words hearers understand. Bob` Duffett tells us how to effectively communicate eternity's truth in contemporary times."

—*Leith Anderson*
Wooddale Church, Eden Prairie, Minnesota

"Bob Duffett gives a clear view of today's seekers who are willing to give a preacher one, perhaps two, chances to reach them. He is not saying, 'Toss out everything you were taught in seminary about preaching!' Rather, he has written a guide for those who want to reach the seeker with the claims of the gospel."

—*Harold Ivan Smith, D. Min.*

"Much preaching today is a monologue delivered by the preacher to churchgoers. Robert Duffett, in clear and convincing language, shows us how to have exciting dialogue with listeners who live and work in a world of secular values. His book will help beginning preachers in sermon preparation and effective delivery techniques. Experienced preachers will discover refreshing ways to add vitality and excitement to their preaching."

—*J. Alfred Smith*
American Baptist Seminary of the West,
The Graduate Theological Union

"Robert Duffett is part homiletician and part paleoanthropologist. His book reveals the 'missing link' between our inherited approach to preaching and the approach that is to be. He does this especially by showing how to connect the message of the Christian tradition with the growing numbers of secular people who don't even know what the church is talking about."

—*George Hunter*
Dean, School of World Mission and Evangelism
Asbury Theological Seminary

"Every minister has a responsibility to faithfully present God's truth in a culturally relevant way to those in the household of faith and to members of the surrounding community. *A Relevant Word* expertly and practically provides the church leader with everything needed to reach people in today's culture with the timeless message of Christ. Bob Duffett provides valuable research and a worthwhile methodology for preparing and presenting the gospel message in the twenty-first century. His insight and pragmatic research will enhance the speaking skills for those interested in making a difference."

—*Doug Fagerstrom*
Calvary Church, Grand Rapids, Michigan

"To my mind, the most significant thesis Duffett advances is that our society has changed so much and so fast of late that preachers are facing an unforeseen challenge: learning to be missionaries to the generation that has been born after them. It is my observation that pastors have generally been trained to preach to audiences with which their theological mentors dealt—often audiences that are no longer living. *A Relevant Word* alerts today's pastors to the reality that the great truths of holy scripture—as previously preached—may not connect with members of the rising generations which they aspire to reach. This timely and helpful book is a manual on how to bring the Good News within reach of a generation of seekers."

—*Carl George*
Church Growth Consultant

A Relevant Word

Communicating the Gospel to Seekers

Robert G. Duffett

Judson Press ® Valley Forge

A Relevant Word: Communicating the Gospel to Seekers
© 1995 Judson Press, Valley Forge, PA 19482-0851

Library of Congress Cataloging-in-Publication Data
Duffett, Robert G.
   A relevant word : communicating the Gospel to seekers / Robert G. Duffett
      p. cm.
Includes bibliographical references.
ISBN 0-8170-1233-8 (pbk. : alk. paper)
   1. Communication—Religious aspects—Christianity. 2. Preaching. 3. Evangelistic work. 4. United States—Social conditions—1980- 5. United States—Moral conditions. I. Title.
BV4319.D84 1995
269'.2—dc20   95-454

Printed in the U.S.A.

95 96 97 98 99 00 01 02   8 7 6 5 4 3 2 1

To David

Contents

Foreword

Contrary to accusations leveled against it by its detractors, the seeker church movement is not about the church becoming contemporary. It is about the church becoming community—the way it was intended to be from the beginning, according to its divine founder. In its essence, the seeker movement is reformist. It rejects corrupt definitions of the church that reduce it to the status of institution, hierarchy, corporation, establishment, or programs. It claims to reach back to the dynamics of the church at Pentecost, to the early tradition that preceded ecclesiastical traditions.

As one who was closely involved with the beginnings of the seeker movement, I can verify that, from its inception, the movement's concern was for the recovery of faith communities that would be inclusive and not rejecting, outreaching rather than ingrown, visionary rather than regressive, humble instead of arrogant, service driven rather than self-serving, upbuilding rather than abusive, participatory rather than controlling. Some of the biblical principles that inspired it were: inclusive community, mutual submission and accountability, community life actualized in small groups, universal use of spiritual gifts, leadership as servanthood, nondifferentiated clergy and laity, gift-specific ministries, plurality of leadership, congregation-based evangelism, and preaching as intelligible discourse.

Over the past twenty years, this new reformation has resulted in a quiet revival that has generated countless congregations composed of previously unchurched people who were reached and transformed into fully devoted disciples of Christ through the instrumentality of biblically functioning communities. Some existing churches that were lying dormant or dead are also being revitalized to become contemporary expressions of the new community that emerged from the old covenant under the impact of Christ's redemptive ministry. This is a movement of the Spirit that will not be stopped.

As important as community is in the purposes of God, there could not be community without communication. Communication is to community what breath is to life. The Scripture, God's communication to humans, is basic to everything the church is and does authentically. No communication, no community. No community, no church.

Both through its forms and in its content, the New Testament makes a passionate plea for God's communication to be transmitted to every culture and to every generation in terms that are meaningful and specific to them. The great Apostle, church planter par excellence, challenged early Christians to communicate the Christian message clearly and sensibly: "Unless you speak intelligible words with your tongue, how will anyone know what you are saying? You will just be speaking in the air" (1 Corinthians 14:9, NIV).

The book you now hold in your hands vibrates with the same passion. Its author, a Renaissance man by reason of his cultural breadth and his range of interests, is deeply committed to making the Christian message comprehensible to the postmodern mind. He has distilled in this work the best insights from several disciplines and brought them to bear on the difficult task of communicating the gospel effectively to the huge masses of unbelievers who surround us and who constitute our primary mission field. There is a lot of talk these days about revival, renewal, and outreach. By following the prescriptions advocated in this book, we could begin to put our message where our mouth is and thus to honor God's historical communication to humans by articulating it credibly to our generation.

Gilbert Bilezikian
Professor Emeritus, Wheaton College
Co-founder, Willow Creek Community Church

Introduction

How does one communicate the gospel to today's seekers? Is there a fresh but not faddish way to communicate to the unchurched and those in the church who find most messages irrelevant, boring, and out of touch with the realities of their lives?

The purpose of this book is to explain how cultural change during this century, and especially since World War II, has shaped people's values, world-views, and expectations. Attitudes about life in general, as well as ministry, church life, and communication, have changed. From these contemporary cultural realities, using homiletics, speech communication, theology, and hermeneutics resources, I present a speaking methodology that considers the experiences, biases, and concerns of those who find most messages and church life irrelevant.

If a person is able to communicate to seekers and the unchurched, I believe he or she will also be able to speak to the needs of those *in* the church. We now know that a Christian home, a good youth group, church involvement, a degree from a Christian college, and a Christian marriage will not shield people from the problems and questions of modern life. Communicators, past and present, have regularly overlooked the impact of culture on the churched. We assumed tomorrow would be like yesterday and have paid a heavy price.

Presently, American religious culture is a paradox. On one hand, over 85 percent of American churches of all denominational and theological persuasions have plateaued or are declining in attendance, membership, and giving. The mainline Protestant denominations (Presbyterian Church USA, United Methodist, Evangelical Lutheran Church of America, American Baptist, Episcopal, United

Church of Christ, Disciples of Christ) were once the largest, wealthiest, and most powerful religious groups in America. They were the "backbone" of Christian America, the moral conscience and spiritual voice of the nation. Yet *Newsweek* magazine reports Stanley Hauerwas, a Methodist theologian at Duke Divinity School, as saying that God is killing mainline Protestantism.[1] Former members of all branches of Christianity, including evangelical, Catholic, Orthodox, Anglican, and charismatic, are also rejecting the church traditions they grew up with. Some conclude that the decline of mainline Protestantism means the triumph of secularism. Interest in spiritual matters and religion must be waning.

Even though spiritual commitment and development cannot be measured by "noses and nickels," membership, attendance, and charitable giving are a commentary on the quality of community. People don't support what they perceive to be meaningless and irrelevant. While thousands of churches are no longer relevant to their own members and are, therefore, unable to attract new ones, about 15 percent of American churches are growing in membership, attendance, and giving. Some now fill the largest buildings for worship in the history of Christendom. Gallup polls reveal a deep interest in religion across America. Contemporary involvement in spirituality and in small-group Bible studies may be at an all-time high. New Age spirituality has thousands of adherents. Addiction recovery groups grounded in an eclectic spirituality have become a growth industry. The sociological data indicates that spiritual and religious interest in America may be *growing*, not declining.

But how does one explain the burgeoning interest in spirituality on one hand, and simultaneous decline of one of the most powerful religious forces in America during the last century? And why have so many left the church of their youth for large, independent churches or become unchurched?

From several possible explanations, this book deals with one: The way the gospel is communicated and the growth or decline of churches and denominations are closely linked. Most people attending growing churches report that the messages are relevant, interesting, and meaningful. They say that the quality of the messages is one factor that makes their church involvement worthwhile.

But thousands of others leave churches because most of what they experience there, including the messages, seems irrelevant.

Throughout the history of the church, good communicators have renewed, revived, and awakened congregations. Technically, churches cannot be renewed or revived; only people can. However, renewed individuals change congregations and denominations and create new ones. In other words, effective communicators have always been instrumental in making the Christian faith and church involvement meaningful to people.[2]

If effective communicators helped renew and revive churches in the past, I believe renewal can happen again. But we in the church must be honest about our failure. The burgeoning interest in spirituality and the simultaneous decline in church attendance present a stinging critique of the type of Christianity and messages we've presented. The evidence is clear. It is time to change how we communicate!

At the outset, let me state the many weaknesses of this book. First, I stumble at the gate in perhaps the most fundamental way. I scarcely mention the theological goal or purpose for communicating the gospel. Communicating, or preaching, the gospel is instrumental in reaching two ends: to bring seekers to faith in Jesus the Christ and to create, restore, and nurture community. The type of community in view is biblically defined, characterized by love, justice, inclusion, acceptance, service, hope, joy, and encouragement. They are lofty ideals for community but are ones that God wants for the world and ones that communicators must affirm. The only excuse I have for such a lacuna is that I am planning a book that will spell out a theology of communication and ministry to seekers. In that work I will consider the link between communication and community, community and the institutional church, and the institutional church and seekers.

Second, I scarcely mention the importance and role that other church ministries, including worship, drama, music, liturgy, small-group ministry, Christian education, and pastoral care, play in reaching seekers. This is a glaring omission but an intentional one. I acknowledge that a total package of ministries and a well-defined philosophy of ministry is necessary in order to reach seekers. We communicators cannot expect to reach seekers by merely following my methodology in our messages. We must be part of the church's leadership team that develops, revises, or changes ministries that will be relevant to seekers. While much has been written about worship renewal, small-group ministry, drama, contemporary music, pastoral care and counseling, and the church in the midst of cultural change, to date, no one has made a systematic attempt to write a book on speaking to seekers. This book is an attempt to fill this gap and should be put alongside the other books and videotapes on contemporary ministry. I hope its specific focus will provoke discussion, provide practical help, and contribute to the growing literature on how to minister to seekers.

Third, the speaking methodology presented is an implicit critique of past preaching traditions and present church culture. I teach preaching. Much of my graduate work was in theology and communication as well as organizational communication. As the endnotes will testify, I am indebted to many from the Christian tradition. However, let me be honest. Past church tradition, vital for one generation, strangles the next. Creativity and cultural sensitivity are relegated to the sidelines by our church traditions. Past agendas become present priorities. In the process, the unique needs of seekers are not addressed.

I do not suggest that contemporary communicators should dismiss the past. Rather, we should seek to retain for seekers what Gilbert Bilezikian calls "the tradition behind the tradition" (see chapter 4). The role of church tradition is to guide but never lead in developing contemporary church ministries and speaking methodologies.

Fourth, the first three chapters deal with history, sociology, and cultural analysis. The reader may wonder what in the world this has to do with communicating the gospel! These chapters spell out in broad strokes why and how our culture is changing. They demonstrate why our era is unique in world history. It is precisely these cultural changes that have created a generation of seekers. Those already familiar with this sociological and historical data may want to turn immediately to chapter 4, where I begin to lay out a method of communicating the gospel to seekers.

Several terms in the book need to be defined. I am a professor of theology and communication. I teach preaching, and this book is targeted to those who stand up every week and try to speak for God. I respect them. I, too, do this every week. However, the term *preaching* is a "turnoff" for many seekers because of past experiences. It is associated with guilt, narrow-mindedness, rules, and all the joy of a bone-chilling mid-January Monday morning. After all, when seekers grow defensive they often say, "Quit preaching at me," or "Don't preach me a sermon."

I prefer to use the term *communicating* rather than *preaching* the gospel. The result is a message rather than a sermon. This book will be useful to anyone who publicly seeks to communicate biblical teaching: youth pastors, Bible study leaders, debaters, and speakers from parachurch groups.

From my perspective, **seekers** are not just baby boomers returning to the church because midlife crises, increasing midriffs, or inability to wear regular-sized Levi's sends them on a spiritual quest. Rather, seekers are those asking ultimate questions due to the ennui of postmodern life. They may be churched or unchurched. Those of us who "hang around the church" have failed to recognize that there are thousands of seekers who are church members and regular attenders who sit next to us. They may be on the verge of changing churches or leaving the church permanently; our messages are simply not addressing their pain, concerns, and questions.

Unlike churched seekers, the unchurched left long ago. But in recent years, they have been experiencing an awakening to things of the spirit. Religious questions, issues, and concerns are becoming more important and can no longer be ignored. Therefore, the term seeker defines anyone asking fundamental religious questions who has not found or is not finding the institutional church relevant to his or her quest.

Throughout the book the reader will become acquainted with **George and Helen Betz** and their children, **Raymond, Barb, and Susan**—a typical American family. The lives of Raymond, Barb, and Susan profile millions of seekers in America. Social, spiritual, and internal dynamics of the last thirty years have conspired to turn these once-faithful church members and attenders into seekers.

Their struggle with Sunday morning messages is similar to that of a growing number of seekers. They once were vitally connected to the church. Through their lives the reader will experience the thoughts, feelings, perspectives, and pain of seekers.

The **gospel** is the Good News that in the life, teachings, death, and resurrection of Jesus, God offers acceptance, redemption, healing, empowerment, community, and hope to all who believe. In its simplest form, the gospel means "Jesus is Lord" over the universe and "Jesus saves." In a more profound sense the gospel is the announcement that the kingdom of God has come in Jesus. A new reality of living has been initiated by Jesus' death and resurrection. The gospel is the ultimate triumph of God over sin, death, and evil and the possibility of new life for individuals, nations, and the entire universe.

I am indebted to many and offer my thanks to the trustees of Northern Baptist Theological Seminary, who granted me a sabbatical leave in 1994. Charles Cosgrove took over my duties as director of doctoral studies and did a great job; Fay Quanstrom edited several revisions of the book. Thanks as well to Barbara Wixon, an incredibly gifted administrator who typed the manuscript and interacted with me on the material. Her insights were particularly helpful. Alfloyd Butler and Susan B. W. Johnson team teach with me, and I have profited from their insights on preaching and communication. Sharon Hoffman, Paul Klipowicz, Jeff Wright, Corey Johnsrud, and members of the Skokie Valley Baptist Church in Wilmette, Illinois, where I serve as the preaching pastor, read and critiqued several chapters. The opinions of the pastoral staff and members of that church may be most important to me since I speak/preach to them every Sunday. If I can't do what I teach and write, then "all is vanity."

Thanks also to my students at Northern Baptist Theological Seminary. This book is for them and others who want to speak with relevancy and reach seekers with the gospel.

Chapter 1

Communicating the Gospel in the Midst of Cultural Transformation

In its first year, *I Love Lucy*, one of America's first situation comedies, was wildly popular throughout America and number one in New York City. Major merchants could not compete with Lucy. In Chicago, department store Marshall Field switched its Monday-night clearance sale to Thursday. A sign in the window explained, "We love Lucy, too, so we're closing on Monday nights." But in the spring of 1952, crisis reigned on the set.

The crisis pitted the producers and writers of the show against the management of Columbia Broadcasting System (CBS) and their sponsors. At the center of the story was Lucille Ball. She was pregnant (in real life). What should be done about this embarrassing situation? The scripts had to be altered, but how? Network executives, at the prompting of sponsors, concluded that a show or two about her pregnancy, followed by cameo appearances, where tables and chairs hid her condition, would be the best course of action. When the "problem" was corrected, they could return to normal.

Others, including her husband (on and off camera), strongly objected. A compromise was struck. Lucy's pregnancy would not be hidden from viewers, but CBS insisted that the word pregnancy not be used. Lucy was not pregnant; she was an expectant mother!

CBS was so careful not to offend American sensibilities that they hired a priest, rabbi, and minister to review all scripts to ensure good taste. During this time Lucille Ball complained that the set looked like a revival meeting with all the clergy hanging around.[1]

Now, fast-forward forty-three years. During the winter of 1995, American Broadcasting Companies (ABC) advertised the show

NYPD Blue with the disclaimer, "Viewer discretion advised due to adult language and partial nudity." In the midst of the baby boom, CBS executives would not permit the term "pregnancy" on television, but by the time baby boomers were raising their own children, adult language and partial nudity were part of prime-time programming.

By anyone's estimation, American culture has changed. These two stories from network television profoundly illustrate that change. But the question is, What is the relationship between change and the way the gospel is communicated?

The stark difference between *I Love Lucy* and *NYPD Blue* did not come about as quickly as one might expect. Two decades ago Alvin Toffler, in an award-winning book, described how our whole society was changing. Old ways in government, business, education, politics, and religion were not working. Ministers in the 1960s, with experience grounded in the 1940s and 1950s, intuitively knew that something was different. Some ministers, and most of society, thought this something was temporary. We'd leave Vietnam, settle the race issue, cut back on industrial pollution, give women a few more jobs, and then society would return to hula hoops, big families, and high church attendance.

But the first sentence of Toffler's *Future Shock* indicates that the clock could not be turned back: "This is a book about what happens to people when they are overwhelmed by change." The key phrase is "overwhelmed by change." If we are being overwhelmed by change, why now? Why didn't this happen in the 1830s or 1920s? Toffler predicted that in the decades of the 1970s, 1980s, and 1990s, millions would face an abrupt collision with the future that would *affect every area of life.* The book was published in 1970 and should be put within social context. The year 1970 was:

- a year after the first moon landing (July 1969);
- a few months after the first Woodstock (August 1969);
- a year after the inferior New York Jets of the American Football League won the Superbowl (January 1969), precipitating a league merger;
- the year of the first Earth Day (April 1970);
- the year of the Kent State and Jackson State killings (1970);

- two years before the Watergate break-in (June 1972);
- three years before the legalization of abortion (*Roe* v. *Wade*) and the end of American military involvement in Vietnam (Paris Peace Accords—January, 1973);
- three years before the Arab oil embargo, a political event that spawned significant social transformations (fall 1973).

In 1970 Toffler predicted that tomorrow would be radically different from today. The title of his book describes a psychological state in which great change in a short time produces "shattering stress and disorientation" in individuals.

Social change has been so profound that even the above events from the 1960s and early 1970s are now remembered as "the good old days." Radio stations throughout the country compete to bring back music that one Chicago station advertises as "the songs you grew up with."

Perhaps the reason so many prefer to listen to the Beatles, the Beach Boys, Chicago, and the Supremes is that the 1960s and early 1970s were a time of hope. Former flower children of the sixties wistfully yearn for a time when change was not so oppressive! But even then, Toffler and Bob Dylan warned that "the times, they are a-changin'."

A decade after the publication of *Future Shock*, Toffler published *The Third Wave* (1980). *The Third Wave* attempts to explain the "whys" of contemporary change by arguing that it was due to a massive shift in the world order. Society in the 1980s was in the process of moving from a second-wave to a third-wave civilization. The book is far from pessimistic. Toffler cites genuine reason for hope. Hope, however, is predicated on understanding what this third-wave shift means for society today as well as the numbing change that accompanied the first two waves.

The First Wave: Agriculture

If our task is to discuss change and its relationship to communicating the gospel, we must go back much farther than the 1960s—almost ten thousand years. First-wave civilization began in 8000 B.C. Before then most humans lived in small, migratory groups.

They fed themselves through foraging, fishing, hunting, or herding. The first great shift (or wave) took place with the rise of agriculture, which became the first turning point in human social development.[2] Agriculture, unlike herding, necessitated settlement because land was cultivated. The economy was local and somewhat self-contained. Craftspeople manufactured goods for the needs of the community. First-wave civilization emphasized place rather than mobility. The effect was an entirely new way of life and the development of a new civilization.

The Second Wave: The Industrial Revolution

First-wave civilization lasted almost ten thousand years. It ended abruptly in the middle 1750s with the beginning of the Industrial Revolution in England.[3] Technological advances and inventions in England's cotton and iron industries during this period led to rapid change throughout Europe. Those innovations included the coking of coal (1735), the use of coke in blast furnaces (1740), the spinning jenny (1767), the steam engine (1769), the "puddling" process of making steel (1784), and the cotton gin (1792).[4]

The most significant impact of those advances and inventions was not technological or economic. Rather, it led to a wholesale attitudinal shift that affected every aspect of civilization.[5] From Clark Kerr's perspective, the Industrial Revolution was such a social force that it was ". . . more basic, more rapid, and more nearly universal than any earlier transformation."[6] William Faunce puts these technological changes in historical perspective. Surprisingly, there was little technological production change and development from the time humanity discovered how to use tools until the Industrial Revolution—a period of several thousand years.[7] Jacques Ellul asks a penetrating question: Why after several millennia of little production and technological innovation did such technological progress erupt? He provides no satisfactory answer.[8] However, improved navigational instrumentation led to world exploration in the sixteenth century, which made possible the discovery of new cultures and the establishment of trading companies.[9] This ferment produced commercial innovation, which became a small step toward industrial innovation.

Before the Industrial Revolution, agriculture was the chief economic activity of society. The extended family (aunts, uncles, cousins, grandparents) lived in close proximity to each other and formed the chief unit of production. With industrialization, the factory system, rather than the extended family, became the chief unit of production. The factory was a social magnet drawing thousands and creating urban areas from yesterday's small towns and farm fields. Family members left home to work in factories.

The shift from work at home to work in the factory, from small village to city, from owner/operator/craftsperson to large-scale factory production cannot be overemphasized. This change happened relatively quickly. For example, on the eve of the Industrial Revolution in 1760 the population of Liverpool, England, was 35,000. By 1881 it exceeded 500,000. Birmingham, England, grew from 30,000 to 400,000 in the same period. In England, second-wave cultural transformation took less than a hundred years. Or, to put it in perspective, an almost ten-thousand-year economic, cultural, and technological way of life was totally transformed in less than a century!

The Industrial Revolution came to America a century later, where shifts from agricultural to industrial jobs were just as pronounced. In 1860, a year before the Civil War, 59 percent of the American labor force was engaged in agriculture, fishing, or forestry as compared to only 20 percent in industry. By 1950, 12 percent of the labor force was agricultural, 33 percent industrial, and 53 percent service.[10] The U.S. Department of Labor and U.S. Department of Commerce calculated a 128 percent increase in the total number of jobs in America between 1900 and 1960 while there was a 54 percent decrease in farm employment. At the same time blue-collar employment increased 133 percent.[11] Second-wave industrialization radically shaped the labor force.

Social transformation from agricultural to industrial employment was cross-cultural whenever second-wave industrialization occurred. In the early 1950s 5 percent of the United Kingdom and 12 percent of the American population were engaged in agriculture, as opposed to 53 percent of Nepal's and 80 percent of Iran's working population.[12] Second-wave industrialization had not yet reached Nepal and Iran.

Second-wave civilization produced smokestacks and mass production as a way of life. Canals, railroads, highways, and air transportation fed the factories and delivered goods to consumers. Only one year into the twentieth century, the world's first billion-dollar corporation was founded—the United States Steel Corporation (U.S. Steel). For most of the twentieth century the slogan "as strong as U.S. steel" was a confident assertion about the quality of the steel, the strength of the company, and the glorious and ever-expanding future of second-wave civilization.

The dizzying effect of past change should not be missed. Assuming that a lifetime is about sixty years, as Toffler does, it took about 160 lifetimes (9,600 years) for the first wave to end and the second wave to begin. Within three lifetimes, by 1900, second-wave industrial employment nearly equaled agricultural employment. But the biggest change was yet to come.

The Third Wave: ?

By 1956, in *one lifetime*, the United States became the first nation in civilization in which more than 50 percent of nonfarm laborers were white-collar workers (i.e., in technical or service jobs). In *one* lifetime, American society witnessed the demise of both the first and second wave and the birth of the third wave! The 1950s and 1960s were perhaps the two decades of most rapid second-wave economic expansion. Yet, as John Naisbitt observes, 1956 heralded the end of the second wave. Industrial America was giving way to a new order—the third wave.[13]

Toffler says third-wave civilization has been called the postindustrial society, the global village, or the space age. Naisbitt prefers the term informational society because it designates what people are doing. Since that landmark year, 1956, more people have worked with information than in farming or producing goods.[14]

We now know why there has been such massive social change during the last 30 years. American society is in the midst of moving from a second- to a third-wave civilization. We are experiencing the "labor pains" of this shift. In the early 1980s Toffler estimated that the third wave would be completed in a few decades.[15]

Today Christian communicators are in the "trough between the waves" as society, values, institutions, organizations, and politics are changing. To paraphrase the apostle John, our whole society does not yet appear as it one day will (1 John 3:2). Very little appears as it shall be in institutional or personal life when the third wave is complete. Nor can we know how it shall be.

Toffler's helpful paradigm should not be pushed too far. As he points out, during first-wave civilization early forms of mass-production factories existed in ancient Greece and Rome. Oil drilling may *not* have begun in 1859 at Titusville, Pennsylvania, but on a Greek island in 400 B.C. or in Burma in A.D. 100. Long before billion-dollar U.S. Steel, there were trading companies in Europe and extensive bureaucracies in Babylon and Egypt.[16] On the other hand, the decal A.N.F. on the helmets of the University of Iowa football players of the mid-1980s attests to the importance of agriculture even as the third wave eclipses the second. A.N.F. stands for America Needs Farmers! Those of us who like to eat agree.

The issue is not the importance or future of industry or agriculture. Both will be part of third-wave civilization. The issue is the radical shift in such a short period of time. There simply are millions *fewer* industrial and agricultural jobs today than even two decades ago. If Christian communicators see these changes only in economic or social terms, it is doubtful that we will effectively communicate Christian truths. This massive economic restructuring has so changed the present and future that old methods, ways, and perspectives simply cannot deal with present realities. Economic changes lead to employment shifts that affect cultures, thus effecting religious and value shifts. Before discussing specific cultural changes, I will use a personal reflection to illustrate the impact of these changes on a specific group of people.

I grew up near a classic second-wave, medium-sized city (Youngstown, Ohio), and graduated from high school on a warm June afternoon in 1972. As I received my diploma, I still wore bandages from a minor accident I'd had at a well-paying, after-school, second-wave factory job. The American economy was strong. The local General Motors plant, one of the largest in the world, was hiring, as were many local steel mills, including U.S. Steel and Youngstown Sheet and Tube. A job in the steel mills was a ticket to the middle class, regardless of one's race, economic background, or education. The wages were so good at General Motors and the steel mills that I often debated my father, a high school principal, about the merits of a college education. I relished comparing the difference between a principal's salary and a mill worker's pay. If I "worked the mills," I would make more money at age twenty than my father did at age forty-seven.

The Youngstown area boasted one of the heaviest concentrations of steel making anywhere in the world. During the cold war, Youngstown people knew they were a prime Soviet Union missile target. As one steel worker put it, "Get rid of us and they won't have anything to fight a war with."

Reluctantly at first, I did go to college. But every summer I returned to "the steel valley," as the area was called, to make "big money" at a rivet mill, a tube mill, or at one of the steel companies. At the rivet mill I watched trains slowly lumber, carrying molten steel on special cars from the U.S. Steel mill in Youngstown to the U.S. Steel McDonald Works for rolling and finishing. Millions of dollars of liquid steel traveled on those tracks. As molten steel was transported, it illumined the night sky, and the slogan "as strong as U.S. Steel" remained proverbial.

The mills never closed, trains never stopped, and time-and-a-half overtime pay was expected. Life revolved around the mills. Blast furnaces roared. Ash coated cars for miles around. Smog choked everyone in the valley as sulphurous smoke filled the sky. If the world was leaving second-wave industry behind, this news had not reached Youngstown or similar second-wave cities. But somewhere between 1972 and the end of the decade the encroaching third wave caught up with Youngstown. By the early 1980s both U.S. Steel plants and two Youngstown Sheet and Tube plants, as well as other steel mills, closed. Plants hiring in 1972 were plants closing in 1980. Thousands of people were out of work. Today the rusting hulks and smokeless stacks against a blue sky testify to a bygone era.

The closing of the mills changed much of the culture for the people in Youngstown—relationships, work, leisure, and trust in industry. Routines changed. Income fell. Tax revenue decreased. Older workers were forced to retire. Younger workers relocated in search of jobs. Churches were filled with those experiencing the numbing effect of job loss. The mills were so important to the people of Youngstown that a group of clergy members tried to reopen one of them.[17] The story of Youngstown is one that also played in Buffalo, Detroit, Bethlehem, Allentown, and all cities built on second-wave economies.

It still may not be clear why a first chapter on communicating the gospel spends so much time on economic sociology. Perhaps you are asking, "Shouldn't Christian communication be above the 'waves' of social change, timeless, focused, and uncorrupted?" I am persuaded that such a question precisely identifies the problem. Regardless of denominational background or theological position, every Christian communicator rides the economic and social waves of the times. As human beings we are part of the society we seek to serve.

Further, Christian communicators must understand the impact that institutions have on those we are trying to reach. Institutions direct and benefit as well as crush our lives. As Robert Bellah points out in *The Good Society*, American preoccupation with individualism means we have developed very little ability to see how institutions affect individuals.[18] If a person succeeds, that person receives credit regardless of who or what helped him or her to prosper. However, failure is always seen individually. It must have been *his or her* fault. The shift from a second- to third-wave economy has produced massive personnel restructuring across corporate America. This institutional change has left many people hurt, stunned, and cynical.

Singer Billy Joel articulates the human pain of economic shift in a song titled "Allentown," which tells about factories closing and the reality of standing in unemployment lines. Even the movies *Wall Street, Country, Roger and Me*, and *All the Right Moves* echo this theme. Many people in our churches seek spiritual guidance and support during such massive economic and social shifts. How does one speak to these people without understanding the psychological pain as well as the social reasons for it?

George and Helen Betz, both seventy, live a life different from their three children. Frankly, they are confused. They don't know whether life is better now or was better back in the 1950s when they raised their children. Both come from German immigrant families. Their grandparents came to Iowa to farm. George and Helen were born and raised in the same small town. They went to the same German Baptist church and graduated together from the same public high school.

Farm work was backbreaking. During the Great Depression they were robbed of their childhood; all family members had to work so they would not lose the farm to the bank. But in the midst of their hardships, their Baptist church provided an oasis of refreshment. No matter how tough things were, whether the bank was ready to foreclose or farm prices were too low, Sunday morning and Wednesday evening were not far away. Hymn singing, listening to the sermon, and praying together restored their souls. No one asked if church was relevant. If it had anything to do with church, it was relevant! If, perchance, someone was bored, the problem was with that person, not the church!

During high school George and Helen knew they would marry one day. But on December 7, 1941, their plans, lives, and future were forever changed. Although George could have qualified for an agricultural deferment, he enlisted in the Navy the next day. That week he asked Helen to marry him. They were married before he left for the war in the Pacific. Their first child, Raymond, was born in 1943.

The war allowed George time to ponder his future. He decided farming was not for him, so after he was discharged from the Navy in 1946 he moved his small family to Detroit. He bought a home in a Detroit suburb and got a job at a General Motors assembly plant. He worked at the same plant for the same company for thirty-five years, retiring in 1982 as head of the machine shop. He always believed that General Motors valued the work ethic and mechanical abilities of farm boys.

After moving to Detroit, George and Helen had two more

children—Barb in 1949, and Susan in 1954. George and Helen's life has been very different from those of their children and grandchildren. George and Helen have been married for more than fifty years; they've lived in the same home since moving to Michigan. George worked in the same plant for thirty-five years, and they've belonged to the same Baptist church since 1947. Their children lived in the same house all their growing-up years and attended the same church and the same public schools. But, as we shall see, this second-wave civilization was markedly different from third-wave civilization.

Chapter 2

The Creation of a Seeker Culture

Raymond Betz, George and Helen's oldest child, was born in the midst of World War II. He was almost three years old before his father held him. He became the typical oldest-child success story. With a double major in electrical engineering and math from a state university, he quickly saw that his future was in the emerging field of computers. His first job out of college in the middle 1960s was with a computer firm. His hunch was correct; hitching his wagon to the computer industry has proved to be an exhilarating ride. His thirty-year career in the field has meant eleven relocations and five company changes. He has lived in Minneapolis (twice), Chicago (twice), Detroit, Dallas, Los Angeles, Denver, the Raleigh/Durham area, and the San Francisco Bay area (twice).

For the first fifteen years, job changes and relocations were due to Raymond's success in climbing the corporate ladder. Almost monthly some headhunter called about a position that was "made for him."

During the last fifteen years, job changes and relocations have been due to survival. In most cases he's left before becoming a victim of downsizing, or as upper management likes to say, "right sizing." His cynical theme has been, "Better git while the gittin' is good."

Raymond's father can't understand all this moving around and leaving a perfectly good job. He has pleaded for him to stay loyal to the company. George has often said, "Raymond, if you're loyal to the company, they will be loyal to you." After seeing thousands of people let go, some escorted out of the building by security guards after twenty years on the job, Raymond thinks his father is out of touch with contemporary corporate reality. Through painful experience Raymond has concluded that loyalty extends only to himself and his family. So far he's been lucky. He's always gotten another job before the "ax fell." Those who were loyal to the company are now unemployed. Hence, when he sees a better deal, he takes it, and the family is forced to move. All of his job changes and relocations have taken him to urban areas.

There was a time when loyalty to the company was rewarded. The plants, mills, and mines of second-wave civilization would eventually rehire those they laid off. Those who were loyal to the company and stayed in the community were rewarded by being rehired. But that day is long gone and continued urbanization and job transfers have become the norm in corporate America. Contrary to what his father thinks, Raymond is no different from millions of Americans. Urbanization, with its concomitant lifestyle options, is one of four social transformations (along with immigration, family permutations, and the changing role of women) that have produced, in the words of Wade Clark Roof, "a generation of seekers."[1]

Urbanization

Urbanologist Ray Bakke says urbanization is one of the most widespread social phenomena of the twentieth century.[2] There is a link between urbanization and second- and third-wave economies. The Industrial Revolution accelerated urbanization. During first-wave society the economy was local and self-contained. Craftspeople supplied local needs. Farmers used local or regional markets.

The Industrial Revolution brought about the radical new work patterns of the factory system. The factory was not only a workplace but also a primitive research-and-development laboratory. Each technological innovation provided greater wealth and incentive to innovate. The factory provided jobs in which people were paid substantial wages (for that time) to do monotonous and dangerous work. Factories were built near essential raw materials, villages, small cities, or trading centers. They became magnets, quickly drawing people from agriculture and transforming small towns into cities.

In a little over 150 years, the factory transformed the demographics of the world. In 1850, only four cities in the entire world had a population of over 1 million people.[3] By 1900, within one lifetime, twenty cities in the world had a population of 1 million or more. At the turn of the twentieth century, world population was estimated at more than 1.5 billion. By 1970, the world population had more than doubled to 3.5 billion. Cities with populations of more than 1 million people (megacities) increased eightfold to 161 megacities. Estimates suggest that the world population will increase to 6.2 billion by the year 2000. Cities with 1 million people will increase threefold to 433 megacities. Urban population growth has far exceeded general population growth. While there has been a sixfold general population increase, megacities increased twentyfold.[4] Expressed in percentages, 9 percent of the world's population was urban in 1900. By the year 2000, 50 percent of the world's people will live in urban areas.[5]

Table 1

Megacities (more than 1 million people)

Year:	1900	1970	1980	1990	2000
Number of Megacities:	20	161	227	340	433

Source: David B. Barrett, "Annual Statistical Table on Global Mission: 1991," *International Bulletin of Missionary Research* 15 (January 1991)

The key question for communicators is: What does the rise of urbanization mean? No doubt there are multiple meanings—economic, environmental, social, and educational. Ralph Turner speaks about the interpersonal effect of urbanization. He uses the term "urban association" to describe a style of human interaction created by urbanization. The nature of urbanization causes people to associate with many different kinds of people. Jobs bring people together. The result is increased exposure to diversity in values, lifestyles, and world-views. However, relationships are generally superficial. Long-lasting relationships of emotional depth are replaced with limited-involvement, impersonal relationships. There is a contrast between the nature of relationships in an urban versus a rural setting. Generally, in smaller rural communities, one experiences more frequent contact with fewer people. Relationships are characterized by greater emotional depth. Roles are more defined and behavior prescribed.

Suburban interpersonal relationships are more impersonal than rural or urban. William McCreary, director of the public opinion laboratory at Northern Illinois University, observes that suburbs simply don't have as many people as some city blocks, and friendship is often a matter of odds. Thomas W. Smith, director of the general social survey in the National Opinion Research Center at the University of Chicago, notes a trend toward less interaction with neighbors in the suburbs.[6]

Raymond Betz's relocations have come with a price. Divorced from his first wife, he is remarried with two children from the second marriage. To George and Helen, their son and his family appear rootless. They have few friends and little involvement in their community. This, Raymond's parents believe, along with the relocations, led to the breakdown of the first marriage. They were shocked when they discovered that Raymond did not even know the names of his next-door neighbors. What a difference from their suburban Detroit neighborhood where everyone knows everybody, even the names of the dogs and cats.

This is not to say that all urban/suburban relationships are impersonal and shallow or all rural relationships are like those portrayed on *Little House on the Prairie*. However, the impersonal character of urban relationships increases lifestyle options because it offers greater anonymity and places less emphasis on religious, sexual, and personal conformity. Urbanization helps destroy localism and tradition.[7]

Although Turner's observation about increased lifestyle options due to urbanization is helpful, I think it needs to be more clearly focused. Localism and tradition are not eliminated in urban America. Rather, urbanization provides more choices. In any major city there is a plethora of local traditions. The urban environment does not destroy these, but rather clusters multiple local traditions, which people may choose or adapt to their taste. Behavior, affiliation, and values are chosen, not prescribed. They may be discarded or altered. An urban environment offers choice, anonymity, and complexity.

In the smaller towns of Europe and America, the church had a competitive advantage. In many locations it was the only meeting place besides the saloon. This has radically changed. The urban and suburban church is now thrown into the marketplace. The Christian faith, lifestyle, and church now provide only one world-view, community, and institution among many. The appeal of church tradition, developed primarily during a rural era, is limited in an urban environment. Opinion polls suggest that church tradition is no longer a compelling force, even for those who are part of it. In fact, one can say that church tradition is meaningless to those outside it. Urbanization and the nature of urban relationships force the church to rethink its tradition and how ministry is done.

Gabriel LeBras studied the impact of urban life on the religious practice of Bretons who moved to Paris in the 1930s. Brittany was a strong Catholic area and Bretons scored highest in France on any indicator of religious commitment. But something changed when residents of Brittany moved to Paris. They simply walked away from their faith. This change was so startling that LeBras postulated that some magical piece of pavement lay in the railroad station where Bretons arrived in Paris. It somehow turned them from good Catholics to agnostics or at least nonpractitioners.[8]

The experience of Bretons was similar to thousands of Catholics, Protestants, and Jews in Europe and America. Paris, like all cities, provided a cafeteria of lifestyle choices. The religious traditions of Bretons no longer fit the Parisian context. Parisian lifestyle choices were more appealing than the local lifestyle choices of Catholic Brittany. A popular American song of the World War I era expressed the dilemma, "How ya gonna keep 'em down on the farm after they've seen Paree?"

The Long Shadow of Immigration

At first glance it might seem incongruous to link immigration with contemporary Christian communication. Immigration explains our grandparents' identity. We recall it from family gatherings, holidays, weddings, and funerals. What possible relevance could considerations about immigration have for contemporary church life?

The culture of any group is derived from its language, values, arts, laws, geography, natural resources, technology, religious institutions, and political organization. All are developed and shaped by human beings and integrated into business, church, and state. Through these institutions, culture shapes and influences persons. It then becomes heritage, which is modified and passed on to successive generations. Our present American culture and church life simply cannot be understood apart from the story of immigration. America is less a melting pot than a tapestry where separate, distinct cultures add to, change in small measure, and then assimilate into the culture. Depending on their number, they both shape and are shaped by the mosaic of American culture. Oscar Handlin may have said it best. As a historian he tried to write a history of the immigrant in America, only to discover that immigrants *were* American history.[9]

Almost seventy years ago H. Richard Niebuhr sought an explanation for denominations and the ethical failure of the divided church. He was unconvinced that denominations resulted from theological diversity. As his search moved from theology to history and sociology, one of his conclusions was that the immigrant church was a major sociological reason for the rise of denominations in American society.[10] This should be expected since his book was published within two decades of massive immigration to America. What, perhaps, is surprising is that Roof and William McKinney, in *American Mainline Religion: Its Changing Shape and Future*, call attention to European immigration as a continuing and contemporary force in American religious life! The central thesis of this book, published in 1989, is to demonstrate how contemporary change is altering religion in America—especially mainline religion. Yet, despite this change, European immigration of two or three generations ago still casts a long shadow on many of America's churches.

The U.S. government estimates that from 1820 to 1973 more than 46 million people emigrated to America. Of this number, there were 35.6 million from Europe, 2 million from Asia, almost 8 million from Canada, Mexico, and South America, and almost 500,000 from other countries.[11] These figures do not include forced immigration due to slavery. Accurate figures of African slaves to America are difficult to determine. In 1861 Edward E. Dunbar estimated that almost 14 million slaves were forcibly transported to the New World between 1600 and 1800. In 1969 Philip Curtin revised these figures. He estimated that 9,566,110 people were coerced into coming to America between 1451 and 1870. Neither figure includes those who were killed while resisting capture in Africa or who died in transport, which some estimate to be as high as 50 percent.[12] Whatever the exact figures, they are staggering.

In 1819 a law was passed requiring the numeration of all immigrants. In the first decade of federal record keeping (1821 to 1830) 143,000 immigrants came to American shores. The numbers rose steadily to 9 million in the first decade of this century. Restrictive immigration legislation (1917, 1921, 1924—the Johnson-Reed Act) virtually banned Asians and limited those from other countries.[13]

Immigration has not stopped but has changed. With the 1943 congressional repeal of the 1924 Oriental Exclusion Act, many of today's immigrants are from Asian countries. The impact of the new immigration patterns is already being felt. The U.S. Bureau of Labor Statistics predicts that:

- Hispanics, Asians, and other nationalities will increase much faster in the labor force than African Americans or European Americans; and
- by the year 2005 the number of Hispanics in the workforce will equal the number of African Americans.

Current patterns of immigration will continue to influence the American society and church. However, past immigration *still* influences much of contemporary church life. Despite vast cultural differences among immigrant groups of the past, their experience was remarkably similar.

But the question for contemporary communicators is, How much of our present church traditions are shaped by our immigrant experience? As Niebuhr pointed out in the first half of this century, and as Roof and McKinney confirm for the last decade of this century, immigrant church tradition is alive and well. In the supposed melting pot, ethnic heritage still plays a prominent role in the denominations. Founded by the British (the English, Welsh, Irish, and Scots), the Episcopal and Presbyterian churches are still predominantly British-ancestral in membership. Formed in 1957 from the largely British Congregational Christian Church and German Evangelical and Reformed Church, the United Church of Christ remains almost two-thirds Anglo-Saxon. Then and now, the Lutheran church is overwhelmingly German and Scandinavian while the Reformed denominations remain Dutch and German (74 percent). Almost 75 percent of Catholics are from German, Irish, Italian, Slavic, or Hispanic background.[14] Most members of African American denominations (Church of God in Christ, National, Progressive, and American Baptist) trace their history via slavery to Africa. Evangelical denominations reflect America's ethnic mosaic better than most denominations. Many, however, were at one time closely identified with an immigrant group.

These statistics suggest that immigration may play a more significant role in contemporary church life than we realize. We may be more tied to the past than we want to admit. The service might be in English but it imitates an order used 100 years ago in another language. Hymns written 150 years ago in Germany are still sung, but in English. Both lyrics and tune come from a completely different culture and period. The church sign may be in English, but, inside and outside, the building looks like those in central Europe. Many older members have a warm feeling about the building. Not only did they help build it years ago, but it reminds them of the church of their youth in the Old Country.

The tie to the old is tighter than we think and this presents a problem. When a local church cannot transcend its long shadow of immigration, how will it meaningfully speak or minister to contemporary American culture? Today large numbers of Americans *cannot* identify their own ancestry and *do not* report a meaningful ethnic identity apart from being American.[15] The conflict is apparent. What meaning does an Americanized service from the Old Country have for someone who has no association with the Old Country?

Most members and regular attenders of Presbyterian, Baptist, and Catholic churches probably are not aware that present worship and speaking styles reflect an immigrant past. In fact, older members feel that most churches have compromised their heritage far too much. As one older Swede lamented, how impoverished the church has become since "they" got rid of the 5:00 A.M. Christmas Julotta service! But ask a newcomer about the German, Polish, Scandinavian, or Irish identity of a particular church. In many cases, especially if the person does not come from that ethnic group, she or he will find it quite pervasive—subtle, but definitely present.

Contemporary communicators must never say that celebrating or affirming ethnic heritage is wrong or that speaking, worship, and ministry styles from the past are bad. However, they are limiting. A church may celebrate and affirm its ethnic heritage, but don't be surprised if membership and attendance continue to decline. If people are not part of the heritage, what does it mean to them?

Christian communicators must recognize the serious conflict between one aspect of the social legacy of urbanization and one aspect of the social legacy of immigration. Roof and McKinney's data demonstrates the continuing presence of the ethnic character of many American denominations. This ethnic character has influenced speaking, worship styles, and traditions as well as ministry priorities. One aspect of the social legacy of urbanization is the importance of choice, anonymity, and relevance for urban and suburban dwellers. Note this conflict. Many of the traditions and priorities of the church hold little meaning for urbanites. Christian communicators are confronted with this conflict and paradox. We come from and often work within a tradition that is irrelevant to large segments of society.

Family Permutations

I often see the phrase "the family church" on a worship program, church letterhead, or sign. The point of the phrase is to underscore the importance of the family and to make a theological statement. The church is trying to communicate support for the family. This is important. Providing support for families should be a priority of every church. Ministry that helps sustain marriages, emphasizes family life, and seriously attempts to teach the Christian faith to its youth is to be encouraged, applauded, and generously supported.

But the phrase raises a fundamental question: What type of family does this church have in mind?

David Elkind uses the term "family permutations" in his book *All Grown Up and No Place to Go.*[16] The term reflects a fundamental change or rearrangement in the family structure. The book describes the unique needs of teenagers growing up in contemporary American society. Elkind clearly sees, as any social observer would confirm, that the family is undergoing radical permutation. Disintegrating family values have brought church and state together for the past five presidential elections (Carter, Reagan, Bush, Clinton). William Bennett's book *The Index of Leading Social Indicators*, modeled after the list of leading economic indicators, catalogs numerous troubled areas in family life. What may have gone unnoticed in Bennett's book is the link between family strife and some of the social, economic, and technological changes of third-wave civilization. A look back will reveal that the family underwent similar stress when society moved from a first-wave to an industrial, second-wave civilization.

Until two hundred years ago, the extended family, with its aunts, uncles, cousins, and grandparents living in close proximity, was the norm. Since most were farmers and travel was difficult, economics kept extended families together. Their subsistence depended on their physical abilities to tend crops and livestock. Work did not separate families. Economic cooperation, no doubt, led to cooperative child rearing. The extended family worked for the whole family and cared for its aged, infirm, and sick. Extended family living should not be construed in romantic or wistful terms, though. Support, love, cooperation, and sharing were necessary for economic and physical survival. However, two points should be made about the extended family.

First, spouses and children held a privileged place. Perhaps it would be more accurate to say that the extended family was a collection of nuclear families (units of parents and their children) that shared economic and kinship ties. Second, as Brigitte Berger shows, the nuclear family was not a creation of the Industrial Revolution,[17] but the rise of the factory system did create a social climate that reinforced nuclear family patterns over other forms.

The Industrial Revolution also led to family permutations. In some cases extended families lived in the same area, worked in the same factories, and kept "kin" ties as in the past. The die was cast, however, for a new family pattern.

For centuries the extended and nuclear family, or as I prefer to call it, an extended collection (based on kinship and economics) of nuclear families, was unrivaled. In the last three decades (1960s to 1990s) other family patterns have emerged. The family is undergoing multiple permutations. At the heart of these permutations is the increase of divorce in American society.

Divorce

Elkind reminds us that divorce was an uncommon experience only a few decades ago.[18] In the 1950s only 2 percent of adults were divorced.[19] Today James Patterson and Peter Kim say that almost 25 percent of adults are divorced.[20] Judy Wallerstein, in the first major longitudinal study of divorced men and women, concludes there are two reasons people divorce: to escape a marriage that has become intolerable for at least one partner and to start a new life. The experience of divorce is a profoundly life-changing event with clear winners and losers.[21] Divorce has given rise to new family living arrangements.

Among the more painful events in George and Helen's life are their children's divorces. It was difficult when Raymond went through his divorce. But it "cut their heart out" when the baby of the family, Susan, announced that she and Brad were divorcing.

Susan was "Miss Everything." She was second in her class in a large suburban Detroit high school, graduating in 1971. She was a cheerleader and homecoming queen, and she constantly lobbied the administration to increase the number of women's sports teams. She was liked by all and envied by many. She matriculated at the University of Michigan in the fall. Ann Arbor, in 1971, was an exciting place. The war in Vietnam, the upcoming national election, the continued racial struggles, and the feminist movement kept the campus in turmoil.

Throughout her college years she was part of an international student movement that aggressively proclaimed that only through faith in Jesus could there be lasting peace. Her education exposed her to ideas and moral and religious questions that her Baptist upbringing and college Christian group could not answer. Her readings of feminist literature caused her to ask many questions about marriage and why so few women were in public ministry in the church.

She met Brad in the Christian group. He, too, was a Baptist. He was a year older, and after she graduated, they were married. Five years later, in the late 1970s, they divorced.

Although over fifteen years have passed, George and Helen still grieve. How could anyone divorce because he or she didn't want to be married anymore? Susan has remained single despite repeated attempts by friends and family to "fix her up with just the right guy." Since college she has worked for the same large pharmaceutical firm. She has been promoted several times and is now a major account representative.

Single Adults in America

As divorce has become more common, the number of adults who are single has drastically increased. In a fascinating book titled *The New Single Woman*, Barbara Schoichet interviews women about their lives, futures, plans, and relationships. She concludes that in America today there is a new type of single woman. She is not a librarian named Marian, a school marm named Mildred, or a woman named Wilma waiting by the phone for a date. Rather, thousands of women are quite happy with singleness. Schoichet discovered that many have little desire to find a mate. They prefer freedom to security. They already have experienced too much TLC from men—treachery, lies, and control. The new single woman does not feel pressure to marry.[22]

Although Susan has not read the book, she is a new single woman. She and Brad, despite their best efforts, could not sustain a marriage of intimacy, passion, joy, and fun. Both decided they did not want to live a lie. Taking control of their lives and futures, they decided divorce was their best option.

Since the divorce, Susan has dated scores of men. She describes most of them as emotionally immature. Although they are going bald and getting fat, they act as if they were in high school or college. She wonders why. Are they like Peter Pan, who never wanted to grow up? Are they going through some psychological development step they missed earlier? Or has life been so disappointing that they want to relive the glory days? Susan is not anti-men and has not ruled out remarriage. But as she looks at who is available, she cynically says her chance at love must have died in the Vietnam War.

Susan's deepest and most profound struggle is not finding a mate. Rather, she wants to find a way to have a baby, preferably without a husband. Her biological clock is ticking loudly. Recently she requested literature from an assisted reproductive technology clinic and an adoption agency. The time for a decision has arrived.

Single Parents in America

The rise of divorce leads to an increase in single parents. In most cases mothers retain primary custody of the children, but not all single mothers are alike. There are at least four different kinds of single-mother arrangements. Some single mothers are teenagers. This is not a new category, but it is a growing one. Many more teenagers are deciding to keep their children. What may have changed most is society's attitude toward teenage sexuality and teenage mothers. As recently as twenty-five years ago, pregnant high school girls (but not the boys that fathered the children) were often suspended or expelled from school. Today some high schools in urban areas provide day care for babies so that teenage mothers can graduate.

Some single mothers are divorced and living with their children. Other single mothers have never been married but have adopted children or have borne them through previous relationships or through artificial insemination. Some single mothers are living with a man who may or may not be the children's father.

Blended Families

The "new single woman" category notwithstanding, most divorced people marry again. This produces a new family configuration, which is further complicated when both partners have children from previous marriages. The stepfamily is the fastest-growing family type in American society. Almost one-half of the children from divorced homes in Wallerstein's study live with stepparents. There has always been remarriage, usually because the spouse died from accident, disease, or childbirth. But second marriages with children provide a new set of problems, issues, and concerns. Wallerstein notes that it is ". . . far more difficult to create a second marriage than a first when children are involved."[23]

Living Together

What was once a poor person's "marriage" has now become a popular living arrangement. The U.S. Census Bureau reports a significant increase in the number of couples who live together without being married. Research from Patterson and Kim indicates that the majority of Americans now view living together as an acceptable lifestyle.[24] Living together does not carry the social stigma it once did. For many couples this is not a temporary commitment but a permanent state. Table 2 illustrates the growth of this type of living arrangement.

Table 2
Number of Couples Living Together

Year	Number of Couples (Millions)
1970	.5 (500,000)
1980	1.6
1990	2.9
1992	3.3

Source: U.S. Census Bureau

The Changing Role of Women

A cigarette commercial of the 1970s is an apt description for a whole generation of women: "You've come a long way, baby." In one generation women received the right to vote (19th Amendment to the U.S. Constitution, 1920) and went on to become bishops, college presidents, and chief executive officers of major corporations.

A closer examination of the historical facts will reveal that first-wave women may have enjoyed more freedom than second-wave women. To be sure, men were the political, ecclesial, and military leaders during both waves. But roles in agriculture-based families showed a more fluid division of labor with little hierarchy. Both father *and* mother were needed to sustain and contribute to family economic life.

In the early years of the Industrial Revolution, women worked side by side with men and children. But the dangerous conditions of factory work led to the passage of labor laws that restricted the role of women and children in the workplace. The factory environment was considered detrimental to their health and moral welfare. One outcome of those laws was an almost wholesale exclusion of women from industrial jobs.[25] As a result, women worked in large industrial companies but in traditional roles—secretary, stenographer, bookkeeper, cook, nurse. Few women worked in the higher-paying white- or blue-collar jobs.

Thus, industrial roles were viewed as masculine and home, family, and nurturance roles were feminine. Dad brought home the money; Mom took care of the kids. For almost one hundred years that pattern was virtually unquestioned. However, within a twenty-five-year period (1940 to 1965) women's roles expanded, constricted, and expanded again. Thousands of men were drafted into the armed forces during World War II. With the largest war in the history of humanity, American industry was pushed to its limit. Women replaced men in the steel mills; shipyards; and tank, airplane, and munitions factories. The result was an efficient, effective, and creative industrial war effort that astonished the world. There were many reasons for America's wartime industrial strength. Part of the credit belongs, no doubt, to the women's workforce, symbolized by the legendary "Rosie the Riveter." But when "the boys" came home, most women returned to the roles of wife, mother, and nurturer—for a time, at least.

Women's roles changed rapidly for several reasons. First, the depression of the 1930s and World War II caused many people to delay marriage and, thus, birth rates fell. Then, with the return of millions of men from Europe and Asia, marriages and birth rates soared. This soaring birth rate became the "baby boom." Third, the

1950s was a period of great economic expansion and prosperity. Families could live in a suburb, own their own home, take vacations, and save for their children's college education on *one* income. Fourth, the government provided generous educational benefits for war veterans. The G.I. Bill enabled thousands to receive a college education, which led to increased prosperity for them.

But as the children of the 1950s grew, many women began to question their limited role. By the 1960s women were entering the workforce in increasing numbers. Twenty percent of all married women worked outside the home in the 1950s. By 1972 the figure had doubled to 40 percent.[26] This percentage has continued to increase into the 1990s. Women now are enrolling in graduate, law, and medical schools in record numbers. They have kept some seminaries from closing as they have boosted enrollment.

Having considered various family permutations and the changing role of women, I return to my original question. If a church advertises itself as the family church, what family is it talking about? Is it prepared to deal with contemporary family permutations—single parents, live-in relationships, two-income married couples? What family system does the Christian communicator have in mind when he or she speaks?

Christian communicators' failure to comprehend changing family dynamics has led to guilt and hiding by many women engaged in the daily juggling of career, family, and marriage. As they look at most churches, they conclude, "They're not my kind of people."[27] As they and their husbands (or boyfriends) listen to the message, they may say of the Christian communicator, "That pastor is out of touch!"

Helen Betz doesn't know whether to envy or pity her daughters. Both are college graduates; Helen had always wanted to go to college herself. In high school she was on the honor roll every marking period. But the depression, war, and young children simply kept her from her dream. Although she has not worked full-time since the beginning of World War II, both Barb and Susan have worked full-time since they graduated from college.

Susan doesn't have children, but Barb has three—two in high school and one in junior high. When she had the children, she took only a two-month maternity leave. Helen doesn't know how her daughter manages her life. She works all day as a high school chemistry teacher, then comes home and does all the housework. (As supportive of Barb as her husband, Dick, is, and as liberated as he claims to be, he hardly lifts a finger around the house.) At least as a high school teacher Barb has summers to catch up.

Few women worked during the 1950s. Now both of Helen's daughters work and it is not even an issue for her granddaughters. They all plan to have careers and children. Helen is delighted that they have educations, career options, and more freedom and choices than she did. But is there too much freedom? Would Susan have left Brad if she didn't have her own career? If women have careers, does it weaken the bonds of marriage or does it mean they don't have to put up with a weak marriage and/or an abusive husband?

Helen pities her daughters because they don't have close ties to place or their ethnic background. Everyone was like family in her German Baptist church in Iowa. Even in their suburban Detroit church and neighborhood everyone was like family. Not now. Her children aren't interested in anything German, and any sense of community seems to have disappeared in big city life.

Chapter 3

Speaking When No One Is Listening: Mandate for a New Method

In the 1950s young lawyers and newly graduated MBAs were advised to join a church because that was where the people and potential clients were. This cynical advice was also good advice. In the fifties, 75 percent of the American population believed that religion was *very* important to them[1] and half said they had attended church during the previous seven days.[2] American religious preference in 1952 was 67 percent Protestant, 25 percent Catholic, 4 percent Jewish, 1 percent other, and 2 percent none. By 1991 religious preference was 56 percent Protestant, 25 percent Catholic, 2 percent Jewish, 6 percent other, and 11 percent none. If religious preference can be put into winner and loser categories, the big winners over the last four decades were "no preference" (450 percent increase) and "other" (600 percent increase). Catholic percentages stayed the same while the losers were the Protestant (over 16 percent decrease) and Jewish (50 percent decrease) categories.[3] Church attendance, while strong compared to other Western nations, dropped in 1991 to 42 percent from 49 percent in 1954. However, church attendance in 1991 was much higher than in 1940 (37 percent).[4]

Although church attendance percentages may be high, those for living one's life from a Christian ethical perspective are low. Patterson and Kim liken the contemporary moral climate to the Old West. Their surveys conclude that "it's wilder and woollier" now.[5]

George Gallup reports similar findings. Seven out of ten adults believe there are few moral absolutes and that ethical behavior must be judged on a case-by-case or situation-by-situation basis.[6] Only 13 percent believe in all Ten Commandments.[7]

I don't believe there has ever truly been a moral consensus in America like many romantically long for. It's too easy to forget slavery and Reconstruction; Native American genocide; the robber barons and the Gilded Age; American involvement in World War I; the rise of the Ku Klux Klan opposing immigration, Jews, Catholics, and African Americans in the 1920s; and other unpleasant historical realities. However, there was a greater moral consensus about private morality despite often hypocritical and secret behavior. Today there is little moral consensus, especially in the area of private morality.

American ministers intuitively know what Gallup, George Barna, and Patterson and Kim have described. If there ever was a moral consensus, we have drifted from it. This drift has spawned countless efforts to redress it, including messages on and calls for revival. The goal of these efforts has been to encourage the integration of America's strong religious interest and participation with the moral content of the faith.

I am convinced that few Christian communicators understand why and how this shift or drift has taken place. Again, if we don't understand how or why, we limit our ability to respond appropriately.

Peter Berger provides insight on the impact of modern Western culture on the moral and spiritual teaching of the church. He argues that modern Western culture has broken down what he calls the "plausibility structure."[8] This term refers to the beliefs, values, ideas, practices, and ways of doing things that society once took for granted. World-view is a synonym for plausibility structure. When there is a uniform plausibility structure or world-view, beliefs, ideas, morals, practices, and ways of doing things are prescribed. The individual has little choice. The plausibility structure determines individual fate.

For the last fifteen hundred years the Judeo-Christian heritage gave Western civilization a plausibility structure that shaped every area of life. Roman Catholic and Reformed teaching have been particularly influential. The lack of a state church distinguishes the American situation from Europe and England. However, the immigrant churches, both Protestant and Catholic; the success of the Methodists and Baptists on the Western frontier;[9] revivalism and the Great Awakenings of Edwards, Finney, Moody, and Sunday; and the strength of parachurch or what Robert Wuthnow calls special-purpose groups,[10] for all their theological, regional, and social differences, perpetuated a plausibility structure that was more similar than diverse. This was reinforced by government, business, and the church.

But the Enlightenment and the Industrial Revolution began to challenge in different ways this uniform plausibility structure. What the Industrial Revolution did to economics, family life, immigration, and urbanization, the Enlightenment did to religious faith, values, and political philosophy. Enlightenment thinking elevated the importance of reason over dogma and creed, emphasized humanistic rather than spiritual concerns, and encouraged social reform and progress through education. Education, it was thought, would bring about reform by sharpening the individual's ability to reason.[11] The combination of urbanization and Enlightenment thought provided individuals with religious, relational, and lifestyle choices that shocked premodern imagination. Many of those lifestyle options were not innovations. But what was once whispered in secret was now practiced openly.

The breakdown of a uniform plausibility structure led to what Berger calls the "heretical imperative." Heretics were easily identified and punished by both the church and state before the Industrial Revolution. Since Europe and America enjoyed a uniform plausibility structure, a heretic was someone who, through word or deed, critiqued the prevailing plausibility structure in some way. Since a strong plausibility structure unified the religious, cultural, and political traditions of society, it provided a background against which anyone who dared raise a challenge stood out. The heretic had nowhere to hide when the powers of church, state, and commerce were unified.

Before Enlightenment values and urbanization shattered the uniform plausibility structure of the West, religious certainty was occasionally ruptured by heresy. After the Industrial Revolution, the Enlightenment, and urbanization, both the plausibility structure and the religious certainty necessary to judge heretics were destroyed. Religious, moral, and lifestyle choices became so numerous, and religious belief so vague and relative, that what once was heresy became one religious choice among many equals.[12] The contemporary religious scene is like a cafeteria where all selections are viewed as equally nutritious—as long as no one gets "sick." In the cafeteria, pluralism, paganism, and syncretism have become the West's new ethical and religious plausibility structure.

Communicating the Christian message was quite easy with a uniform plausibility structure centered on the Christian faith. The Christian message shaped social structures while these same structures reinforced the Christian lifestyle and doctrinal views. The goal of Christian communication was to declare and hand down the tradition. The message was reinforced socially. One did not have to be personally effective or creative since church, state, business, and tradition worked together to keep the plausibility structure intact.

Communicating the Christian message when there was a uniform plausibility structure centered on the Christian faith was like playing a basketball game—using partisan referees—in front of the home crowd, all of whom were cheering for you. How could one fail? But contemporary communicators are faced with a radically different situation. We are playing on someone else's court; the referees are hostile; and the crowd either stays home, leaves early, or cares more about the band. No doubt several are interested, supportive, and rooting for us, but their cheers are difficult to hear.

This, perhaps, is the most difficult challenge. Most of our speaking styles, theology, and Christian traditions come from a time when Western culture was on "the Christian court." Today we speak the Christian message in an entirely new context. We communicate to a different audience, on their court, and without help from social structures. The contemporary situation calls for a major reassessment of how the Christian message is communicated.

What, then, may be done? How should the Christian message be communicated in light of the contemporary situation? From Berger's perspective the goal of Christian communication is to preserve the Christian tradition for contemporary society. He defines tradition as the collected memory of another world that has broken into the reality of everyday life.[13] But perhaps the most important question Berger does not address is, What memory of what world?

The biblical memory or tradition? The memory or tradition of the Reformation? the immigrant church? or the fine points of theological controversy from a previous generation?

Assuming that Christian communicators seek to retain the biblical tradition for the contemporary scene (which will be discussed in the next chapter), Berger argues that we have three options.[14] First, the Christian tradition can be reaffirmed in defiance of modernity. He calls this the deductive possibility. Although Karl Barth is cited as an example, fundamentalists and some American evangelicals may be better ones. Despite the needs, views, and lifestyles of modern culture, with this option the methods and perspectives of the past are the agenda for the future. Since the methods worked in the past, we will make them work now. The problem is not with the church, ministry, or how or what is preached, but with the modern world. The goal of this option is to preserve orthodoxy as understood from a previous generation. Despite its noble goal, orthodoxy is not preserved. Orthodoxy of this type is viewed by the modern world as a model T car. It's nice to look at and is appreciated for its contribution to automobile technology, but it is not taken seriously as a modern mode of transportation. This option fails to confront culture and, rather than maintaining orthodoxy, actually *fails* to preserve it in a culturally relevant way. This approach carries with it the seeds of its own destruction. The theological legacy of a previous generation is made to set the agenda for the present generation. The problem is that the present generation views the legacy as irrelevant and meaningless.

Two years before her divorce, Susan dropped out of church. The trauma of the divorce motivated her to return. Like her brother, Raymond, and sister, Barb, Susan has positive views of the Baptist church of her youth. By any standard, her parents were successful in giving their children faith and Christian moral values. All during their youth they enjoyed going to church. Susan still doesn't need to use the hymnbook; she knows all the hymns by heart.

Several months after the divorce was final, Susan went to a Baptist church like her home church and the one she and Brad attended early in their marriage. After attending this church for six weeks she returned to the ranks of the unchurched. The messages she had heard were particularly irritating. The goal of every sermon seemed to be to answer questions no one was asking, to scold the congregation, or to call the church to return to either the first century or the Reformation period. She concluded that she did not want to be yelled at—life is negative enough—and that if she wanted to learn about history she would take a course at the local college, not go to church.

Berger's second option, the reductive possibility, discards much or most of the Christian tradition that does not conform to modernity or modern moral sensibilities: Babies cannot be born of a virgin. People don't rise from the dead. Demons don't cause illness. Further, individuals decide their morality. The goal of this position is to retain the validity of the Christian faith in the face of religious and secular competitors. However, in the process many theological concepts are discarded or reinterpreted.

Despite the noble goal of this option, what is perceived as helping to maintain the credibility of the Christian message has actually hurt it. What looks like myth from a prescientific era is part of the essential core of the Christian faith. What sustained intellectual belief for one generation well acquainted with the doctrinal teaching of the historic Christian faith provoked unbelief in the next. The intellectual content of this reductive possibility is viewed by many as little more than individual and social justice for which one does not need faith or the church! I believe that much of mainline Protestantism illustrates this option. Too much of the historic Christian faith has been given up. Roof and McKinney predict the continual decline of mainline Protestants in numbers, social power, and influence.[15] Although there are many reasons for this decline, I think the chief reason is that mainline Protestants have consistently modernized the wrong aspects of the Christian tradition. On one hand, they cling to worship and preaching styles, hymnody, and liturgical forms that are irrelevant to most people. On the other hand, they ignore or reinterpret aspects of the biblical tradition that are indispensable to the content and ethics of the Christian faith. Claiming relevance, mainline Protestants have become irrelevant to *their own* people. Roof and McKinney claim that Protestantism has lost members both to the right and to the left. Many have left for conservative churches; many others have left for secularism.[16]

Raymond has had a far different experience with the church than Susan has. Like Susan, however, he and his first wife quit going to church. The excitement of climbing the corporate ladder, relocating, and seeking a more affluent lifestyle left little time or desire for church. Like Susan, his divorce and the resulting questions and pain caused him to go back to a cathedral-type, downtown, mainline, "First" church. He met his present wife there.

Although this church was effective in ministering to Raymond in his time of need, he now has serious reservations about the church. He is emotionally and spiritually torn. Individuals from his Baptist church background would have summarily condemned him because of the divorce. The people at the First church nurtured him. But the messages are merely advertisements of left-wing social and political causes. Accepting of many alternative lifestyles, they offer little more than "do-good-isms." He agrees with most of the views expressed. His father still has not forgiven him for voting for Mondale, Dukakis, and Clinton. As educated, politically aware, and left of center as he is, he still wonders why he needs to come to church for what he calls political speeches. At times he wonders if he is becoming a fundamentalist. At other times he does a quick cost/benefit analysis of church involvement. One does not need church to be involved in political issues. Therefore, why bother getting up on Sunday morning?

But Raymond and his wife still grudgingly trudge off to church—for the kids' sake and out of guilt—the First church was there when they needed a church. Increasingly, however, they find reasons to stay home. Certainly the message is not the only reason. Still, Raymond's analytic mind deals best with cold facts. If the message is one-half of the service, and most messages are poor, where is the value? He and his working wife can invest their time elsewhere.

The third option, the inductive possibility, attempts to rediscover and retrieve the experience embodied in the tradition for a new cultural situation. This is what Bilezikian says is the "tradition behind the tradition." It neither condemns nor celebrates modernity while it attempts to articulate the core of the Christian faith in ways that are understandable today. This option fits the cultural reality of the heretical imperative of modern society. Evangelicals would like to claim they practice this third approach; however, many are not as effective in ministry nor as biblical as they see themselves. The pride of the evangelical movement is its claim of uncovering the biblical tradition and the tradition behind the tradition for today. From my perspective, this boast is more rhetorical than factual. Immigrant church traditions, detailed doctrinal statements, denominational priorities, political alliances, and behavioral codes that reflect the fundamentalist side of the controversy with modernism are evidence that the biblical tradition may not be as binding as evangelicals assume. Or to put it another way, the traditions of evangelicalism have shaped how evangelicals read and understand Scripture far more profoundly than they think, despite loud claims that Scripture is their *only* source of authority. In many cases their tradition has a higher authority than The Tradition behind *their* tradition.

Berger's insights aid our efforts to develop a way to communicate the Christian message to the modern world. The astute observer will note, as Diogenes Allen and many others have pointed out, that we are at the end of the modern world. Philosophers and theologians agree that the ideals of modernity from the Enlightenment have collapsed. Allen lists four modern world-view pillars erected during the Enlightenment that now lie in shambles.

First, it can no longer be maintained, on philosophic or scientific grounds, that we live in a closed universe. Since the Enlightenment, cosmological questions about God have often been ignored. Today scientific questions about why this universe rather than another, why order rather than chaos, and why the universe exists at all beg for theological consideration. As some have put it, "the God question" calls for response.

Second, modern society has failed to find a basis for social morality. Enlightenment thinking assumed that reason and education would lead to a better private and public morality. Quite to the contrary, Enlightenment thinking led not to a more adequate, but to a more chaotic morality.

Third, the experience of the modern world has shown that the Enlightenment assumption of the inevitable progress of humanity was a hoax. Crime, pollution, poverty, racism, and war demonstrate that progress creates as well as solves problems.

Fourth, knowledge may not be inherently good. Advanced knowledge has led to advanced technology. But advanced technology has also been used for evil purposes.[17]

As society moves from modern to postmodern or the third wave, Allen sees this as a potentially positive period if the church is able to rise to the challenge. The collapse of Enlightenment dogma means that ". . . Christianity is liberated from the narrow, constricting, asphyxiating stranglehold of the modern world."[18]

There is no quibble among Berger, Allen, and Toffler. Moving from the modern to the postmodern world means that choice, pluralism, and syncretism still dominate the religious and moral scene.

The postmodern world is forcing Christian communicators to reassess how we communicate the Christian faith. The chief question is: How does one connect with a postmodern culture? Much research has been done to discover what people find meaningful in the church and why people are leaving.

Lee Strobel states the truth clearly. Most people quit going to church because it's boring, predictable, irrelevant, and money seeking, and because they are too busy.[19] Strobel accurately expresses Susan's and Raymond's "beef" with the church, even though both want to become part of a church community.

In Raymond's case church seems to offer decreasing benefits. His children would rather play soccer and football on Sunday. In their suburb, as well as many others, both sports practice and play on Sunday morning. Raymond, his wife, and his children are too busy to tolerate boredom. It's getting tougher to say no to his children's requests to play. He thinks back to his childhood when there were no events on Sunday but church. Times sure have changed!

If Raymond is in the church but on the way out, Susan is outside the church trying to find a way in. Since her divorce she feels guilty about not being a vital part of a church. Every January she determines that this year she will find a church, but her resolution ends in the same way—no matter which church she attends, the messages are virtually irrelevant to her life.

During the week Susan works with some of the most intelligent people in America. Her company and her products are at the forefront of high-tech medicine. In this competitive, male-dominated world,

Susan is effective and successful. But the exterior success cannot cover the interior desires or pain. Her most important desire and ethical problem is that she wants to be a mother but not a wife. Brad was the Christian man of her dreams. They were going to live "happily ever after" and often talked about how many children they wanted and what their names would be. It seemed so natural—love, career, marriage, the baby carriage, and happiness. She wishes her dreams had come true.

Life doesn't always work out the way one wants, however, so Susan has taken control of her life. She reads and rereads the brochures from the assisted reproductive technology clinic and adoption agency and mulls over the economic, ethical, religious, and practical implications of such a decision.

She recently went back to church with high hopes that this time it would be different. The minster was just beginning a six-week message series on Christian family values. Susan was actually excited. Maybe the messages could help her resolve some of the issues regarding single parenting, adoption, in-vitro or artificial insemination, and the lingering guilt she feels about her divorce.

At the end of the series she was disappointed. Nothing was mentioned about single men and women, stepfamilies, divorce, marital discord, or single mothers. She wishes, just once, someone would give a message on people's struggles and pain from a biblical perspective. Is it too much to ask that messages deal with today's concerns and questions?

She's thought about writing to the pastor to express her disappointment in the series. She wants to request a message on "living when the biological clock is ticking." She smiles as she thinks about what church people might think about such a message for a single woman. But she's decided not to write the letter. It's easier to return to being "unchurched."

Barna's research on the unchurched confirms many of Strobel's findings noted earlier. Barna defined the unchurched as those who have not attended church in the past six months. Surprisingly, he discovered that 70 percent of the unchurched have favorable impressions of Christianity and 20 percent claim to be born-again

Christians. When asked to explain why they choose not to attend church, two-thirds mentioned one of the following:

- I am too busy (20 percent);
- I have no interest in being part of the church (14 percent);
- I have had bad experiences with the church (12 percent);
- I have no reason for not attending (19 percent).[20]

Gallup found similar results in the 1978 and 1988 surveys of unchurched America. The chief reasons for people dropping out of church were that they found other activities, moved to a new community, started making their own decisions (young adults), had schedule conflicts, and realized an incompatibility of lifestyle with the church. Specific problems the unchurched had with the church were its concern for money, narrow belief system, narrow teaching on sex and marriage, ineffectiveness in helping to find meaning in life, and poor preaching. Reasons for becoming unchurched or reducing one's involvement with church are not significantly different among whites, blacks, and Hispanics.[21]

Barb, the middle child, did everything right. She graduated with majors in chemistry and education from the Baptist college that her church in Detroit supported. She married a man whose father was a prominent minister in the denomination. She and her husband have been married for more than twenty years and are actively involved in a Baptist church. With two children in high school and one in junior high, she and her husband are youth-group sponsors. Barb has enjoyed a good marriage and a fulfilling career in education and by all accounts has been an excellent mother.

Unlike her brother and sister, she has a positive church experience. But she is presently living in a world of private pain. Her youngest child has Down syndrome. Last year Barb was diagnosed with breast cancer and underwent a partial mastectomy. Her husband only recently found a job after being unemployed for eleven months following a midmanagement downsizing. She often cannot sleep, thinking about her life: Will the cancer come back? Will I be able to beat it or will it kill me? If so, how will the oldest two go to college? Who will watch the youngest? Her husband tries to be supportive, but cancer creates such loneliness, such emotional distance.

There also is little support in her church. Perhaps people don't know what to say or how to say it. They simply ignore the family's child with Down syndrome. There are few people in her church that Barb feels "safe" with. No one allows her to be vulnerable and real with her feelings. This was not always the way it was at church. About five years ago a new pastor came. He is a great speaker; he is relevant and biblical. Even Raymond and Susan like to come to church to hear him when they visit Barb. But a five-year diet of "happy-face" answers for every question and "four ways to happiness" sermons has produced a superficial congregation. The climate is that real Christians don't have real problems. Or worse, if real Christians do have problems and pain, they can quickly overcome them by "doing these steps" or "applying these principles" to their lives.

The problem is that sometimes lists, pep talks and happy-face Christianity works. The hitch is that Barb's cancer is real, and it may really come back. Down syndrome is real. The lack of her husband's employment is a real problem when the family budget is based on two paychecks. These problems are not easily overcome.

Barb will not leave the church. She has too many friends there. But why can't messages deal with the pain of a disfigured woman whose husband no longer touches her? Yes, there is joy in Jesus, but there is sorrow too. Help me make sense of my pain and point me to meaning, Barb pleads inside, and she wonders, Is this too much to ask?

Table 3
Why People Dropped out of Church

1. Found other activities.
2. Moved to a new community.
3. Started making own decisions.
4. Had schedule conflicts.
5. Realized conflict with moral teaching of the church.
6. Found it ineffective in helping find meaning in life.
7. Heard poor preaching.

Source: George Barna, *Never on Sunday: The Challenge of the Unchurched*

Dean Hoge, Benton Johnson, and Donald Luidens studied 532 Presbyterians confirmed in the late 1950s and 1960s in a nationwide random sample reminiscent of the book *What Really Happened to the Class of '65?* [22] They discovered that 52 percent were churched while 48 percent were unchurched. Their definition of the "churched" was members of a church who attended at least six times per year. One finding for communicators is important: The key issue for church attendance is not denomination but "comfort zone." In other words, people want to go to a church where they feel comfortable. Comfortable is defined as a church not too distinct from what they are used too.[23]

Russell Hale adds another dimension. His interviews with the unchurched have convinced him that hosts of unchurched people have heard more bad news than good news from the pulpit. Many have *never* heard of a loving, accepting God. Rather, they've been overloaded with law, guilt, judgment, and rejection.[24] What is important is that these people were once churched. They heard, saw, experienced, and left!

Patterson and Kim's surveys say that confidence in organized religion fell from 49 percent in 1974 to 22 percent in 1989. Of all institutions surveyed (education, the military, the press, television, organized labor) the church showed the most precipitous drop in confidence.[25]

How can it be that Raymond, Barb, and Susan, raised in the church, are all disappointed by what they experience there? In each case the messages evade their struggles, pain, questions, and concerns. Multiply their experience by thousands, maybe millions, and this, perhaps, explains in part why confidence in the church is at such a low ebb. It is certainly ironic that committed Christians have now become seekers.

So What?

The purpose of these first three chapters is to answer the question of why there has been so much social change in the last forty years and to reflect on what these changes mean for contemporary communicators.

In any generation, an individual's life experiences shape his or her view of God, the Bible, and the church. For fifteen hundred years a Christian world-view gave Western civilization a Judeo-Christian perspective on the role of government, the importance of the church, and how people should live their lives. For centuries, millions of people uncritically accepted this comprehensive system of thought and action. There were few rivals.

But the Enlightenment and the Industrial Revolution of the eighteenth century and the resulting urbanization, immigration, family permutations, and lifestyle options shattered the Christian world-view of the West and sent the church scurrying to redefine its ministry and message for a new social order.

Christian communicators find themselves in a cultural quandary. Research survey data consistently demonstrates that large segments of our population believe in God, think religion is important or very important, and pray at least occasionally. Gallup discovered that two-thirds of the unchurched indicated the possibility of their becoming active in the church again.

But the same survey data suggests that much of church culture and tradition bequeathed from a previous generation is dangerously close to becoming irrelevant and meaningless to significant numbers of Americans. Our words sound shrill, negative, condescending, and angry. When we speak of morality we sound narrow, bigoted, and out of touch. Our appeals for money are perceived as self-serving. Our content touches few where they live.

So what is it that seekers like Raymond, Barb, and Susan expect from messages when they come to church? At its most fundamental level, seekers are looking for some anchor or foundation for their lives. Cast adrift in moral relativity and awash with the difficulty of life, seekers look for love, some sense of certainty, and moral direction. Is there something in life that provides direction without being overbearing, wisdom without being dry and superior, and a moral sense without being dogmatic? Is there anything that will last during tough times?

Happily, for seekers like Raymond, Barb, and Susan, the Bible provides that moral anchor and points to a God who loves the world with an everlasting love. Chapter 4 teaches how the Bible can be used to reach seekers. But seekers will not believe unless it makes sense. Seekers like Raymond, Barb, and Susan are bright, articulate, and aware of the world. The content of a message from the Bible must connect to their experience. Messages to seekers must be relevant, meaningful, and interesting from their perspective. Chapter 5, on connection, describes how to connect the Bible to seekers.

Since seekers are so busy and usually allergic to boredom, communicators must learn how to organize messages. Seekers' lives are confused already; they don't need to be confused on Sunday morning. Organization takes the biblical teaching and shapes it in such a way that it connects and is useful to seekers. Chapter 6 lays out a method of message organization that is sensitive to seekers.

Those who speak to seekers need to be authentic and speak with heart, soul, and passion. Unlike churchgoers in the past, seekers know that ministers and Christian communicators struggle with doubt and pain. Therefore, a seeker message does not pretend that the speaker is above the pain. Rather, the speaker shows how the resources of the Christian faith and church help him or her as well as seekers to deal with pain, questions, and problems.

Chapters 7 and 8 deal with the issues of speaking with integrity, heart, soul, and passion. Chapter 9 discusses message planning and selection. Each of the chapters is an important component in the development of messages for seekers.

This book does not presume to deal with all church-related problems, but it does deal with how the Christian faith may be effectively communicated to seekers. One method of communicating that takes cultural realities seriously will be presented. Using this method should help *connect* the *content* of the Christian faith with people "where they live."

Chapter 4

Message Content: Finding an Anchor

If Raymond, Barb, and Susan, like other seekers, are searching for an anchor for their lives, then the first question for contemporary communicators is: What should be the anchor/content of contemporary Christian communication? This is an important question in postmodern society even though it was not an issue for the church in premodern society. The crucial debate in former centuries, when the plausibility structure of society was thoroughly Christian, centered on the role and authority of church tradition to interpret the Bible. Regardless of the viewpoint of the debate, the Christian world-view was proclaimed. Today the question has changed because the church faces the challenge of the heretical imperative: any message content is possible.

Given the religious options of American society, some might attempt to define the content of contemporary Christian communication as "being all things to all people." Mix a little Bible with positive thinking, add in a dash of mysticism, and stir in American civil religion. Another option is to determine content through an analysis of what individuals mean when they speak of spiritual experience. Talk show guests often speak about "spiritual" relationships and spiritual experiences. Some call themselves spiritual but not religious. Few define or elaborate what they mean. Given how "slippery" the terms spiritual and religious are, contemporary communicators could try to understand the nature of spiritual experience and then use this for the content of messages. This option certainly has the advantage of being relevant.

A third content alternative is to reassert church tradition with greater vigor. I critiqued this approach in chapter 3. Those who disagree may think the critique is the problem. The goal for contemporary communicators is not to rid ourselves of tradition but to articulate and live out the tradition better. Therefore, Christian communicators, depending on their tradition, should reemphasize what it means to be Baptist, Assembly of God, Methodist, or Catholic. The advantage of this option is that identity is an important concern for most denominational leaders.

I don't believe that any of the above three options will provide an adequate content base or anchor for contemporary Christian communicators. Option one, syncretism, contradicts the essence of the Christian faith. Option two, understanding spiritual experience, is testimonial. It is interesting and important, but insufficient.

The third option, church tradition, is actually a sociological and historical extension of religious experience. The focus of religious experience is on the individual while church tradition focuses on the communal and the historic. Therefore, if church tradition informs how earlier Christians felt, believed, and lived, it suffers the same fate as option two. It describes but it has no power to prescribe. Furthermore, church tradition has little meaning for contemporary society. Most modern seekers simply don't care what historic Baptists, Assemblies of God, Methodists, or Catholics thought about any issue. Church tradition as the content for contemporary Christian communicators will be perceived as being quaint, irrelevant, and out of touch.

This leaves a fourth option—the biblical tradition, or as Bilezikian likes to say, the tradition behind the tradition. In contemporary culture it is not enough simply to assert the option of biblical tradition. Rather, it must be argued. There are three arguments for the Bible as the content for contemporary communication. First, the Bible claims for itself a unique authority. Throughout the Old Testament, claims are made that God is speaking through the prophet, king, or priest to the people. A. Berkley Mickelsen lists three phrases found throughout the Old Testament declaring God has something to say to the people. These phrases are:

"Thus says the LORD" (e.g., Exodus 4:22)
"The mouth of the LORD has spoken" (e.g., Isaiah 58:14)
"The word of the LORD came" (e.g., Jonah 3:1)
In all cases the prophets or leaders proclaimed God's word and

not their own. God was present in their speech and wanted something to be made known.[1]

The same assertion continues in the New Testament. Jesus underscored the importance of both the Old Testament and his words. New Testament writers followed Jesus' lead. Paul joined by declaring that "all scripture is inspired by God" (2 Timothy 3:16). As in the Old Testament, God worked through the writers of Scripture with the result that the written word reflects divine authority. Peter assured readers that the prophets did not invent their message (2 Peter 1:20-21). Rather, God energized them to write. The last sentence of verse 21 is important: "But men and women moved by the Holy Spirit spoke from God." The passive voice of being "moved" suggests that the Holy Spirit actively engaged the writers of Scripture to provide a document that was God's word through the author's words. This quick overview demonstrates unanimous biblical attestation that the Bible's claim to authority rests on the authority of God.

The second argument for the Bible as *the* content for contemporary communication is the testimony of the church. The church has affirmed that the presence and authority of God comes to the church and world through Scripture. Despite the difference between Roman Catholicism and Protestantism over some books of the Bible and the role and authority of church tradition in interpreting Scripture, the Second Vatican Council links the authority of Scripture to God.

> "Holy mother church, relying on the belief of the apostles, holds that the books of both the Old and the New Testament in their entirety, with all their parts, are sacred and canonical because having been written under the inspiration of the Holy Spirit (cf. John 20:31; 2 Timothy 3:16; 2 Peter 1:19-21, 3:15-16), they have God as their author."[2]

The constitution of the Lutheran Church of America (L.C.A.), one of several Lutheran bodies that joined to form the Evangelical Lutheran Church in America, acknowledges that the Holy Scripture is divinely inspired and that God still speaks through Scripture, thus realizing God's own redemptive purpose from one generation to the next.[3]

The Belgic Confession of Faith, which enjoys wide acceptance in many Reformed churches, says "The authority of Scripture comes not from the church but because the Holy Spirit witnesses in our hearts that they are from God."[4]

The Presbyterian Confession of 1967 speaks about both the interpretation and authority of the Bible. "The Bible is the one sufficient revelation of God in Jesus Christ. Through the Scriptures the church hears God's word."[5]

The United Methodist Confession of Faith says that the Old and New Testaments reveal the word of God "as far as is necessary for our salvation."[6] The most important confession of faith for Baptists is the 1830 New Hampshire Confession of Faith. It influenced the 1925 and 1963 Southern Baptist Convention's Baptist Faith and Message, as well as the National Baptist Convention of America and American and Conservative Baptists. The confession says that Scripture was written by men divinely inspired, but that God is the author. The Bible is the supreme standard by which all human conduct, creeds, and opinions shall be tried.[7]

The Assemblies of God, one of the world's largest charismatic groups, affirms in their Statement of Fundamental Truths that "the Bible is our all-sufficient rule for faith and practice" and ". . . is the inspired word of God, a revelation from God to man."[8]

A word of caution should be raised about statements of faith. They are human and political documents, often borrowed, and usually written in the midst of doctrinal or ecclesiastical controversy. However, whatever the limitations of statements of faith, the above sampling shows a clear consensus concerning the role of the Bible.

The first two arguments for the Bible as the anchor or basis for message content will only convince "the choir." In other words, only those who already believe will find them persuasive. Critical biblical scholarship affirms that the Bible was *not* written by pipe-smoking university professors in tweed jackets. Rather, the authors of biblical books were actively engaged in the community of faith. The Bible was written by community members for the community of God. To "nonchoir" members something seems awry. If biblical authors were from the covenant community (Old

Testament) or the church (New Testament), weren't their writings biased? What credibility is there if the institutional church affirms its own writings and propagandists?

The third, and perhaps the most persuasive reason that the Bible is the anchor or basis of message content is Jesus' own view of the Old Testament. For him the Old Testament was authoritative. He says that he came to fulfill the law and the prophets (Old Testament), not to abolish them. Using hyperbole (see below) he underscores the authority of the Old Testament: "until heaven and earth pass away, not one letter, not one stroke of a letter, will pass from the law until all is accomplished" (Matthew 5:18).

Concerning the New Testament, Jesus committed his teaching to disciples (Matthew 28:19,20), commissioned them to pass on this information, and promised them the presence of the Holy Spirit in all their endeavors. The New Testament Scripture, then, is a written record of Jesus' teachings, authored by his disciples and other church leaders under the inspiration of the Holy Spirit, for the community of faith. The church collected oral and written material from the life and teachings of Jesus and other writings about the church. These written materials were subjected to a rigorous process over a long period of time that determined the authenticity of the document. The result was the New Testament that accurately records Jesus' teachings and the beginning of the church. In this way the New Testament is authoritative for the church, on par with the Old Testament, and therefore is the anchor and basis of contemporary messages.[9]

If the above discussion settles the content issue, by logical extension the role and task of contemporary communicators is settled as well. Our role is to communicate the content of the Bible. To fulfill this role the chief task of contemporary communicators is then to interpret Scripture effectively.

The task of interpreting Scripture cannot be avoided. No church group will permit its pastor to read twenty minutes of Scripture and then sit down. Frankly, I am not aware of any group in any culture at any period in the history of the church that expected its leader to read Scripture during worship without trying to discern what the Scripture was saying to the assembled community. Virtually all groups place a strong emphasis on the teaching ministry during their services. Often this teaching is a public reading of Scripture with relevant comments to the community.

There is almost universal expectation of some contemporary explanation or insight based on a read biblical passage. Whether one looks to statements of faith, the history of worship and preaching, or contemporary expectations of church attenders from the most liturgical to the most charismatic and from the most liberal to the most fundamental, *all yearn for the communicator to connect Scripture to the world today.*

If the Christian communicator accepts this distinct role of communicator *and* interpreter of Scripture, he or she has entered into the world of biblical interpretation. The goal of biblical interpretation is to determine, as much as possible, what the authors meant for the original readers and then to transmit that meaning to an analogous situation in the modern world.[10] The first step is content, which will be discussed here. The second step is connection (the subject of chapter 5).

Christian communicators must be aware of the difficulty of interpreting Scripture. There are many problems between the then and the now. First, there is a radical difference between the postmodern world and the world of the Bible. This discontinuity is so great that some openly question whether "an old book" has anything to say to contemporary concerns. Second, there is a considerable cultural gap between then and now. The Bible was written by and to specific people living in a Hebrew culture and then in a Jewish/Hellenistic environment. Most of the Bible was written at least two thousand years ago in what we now call the Middle East. Most Americans do not understand *modern* Middle Eastern culture. What chance is there to understand a book written in the *ancient* Middle East?

Third, the history of the Bible is distinct and distant from Western and American history. The Bible reflects its culture and historical content. This is not necessarily a problem unless one seeks to communicate biblical content to a culture that holds little value for history—like that in most of America! Fourth, when reading, speaking, or hearing a text, no one interprets with pure motives. I wish we could all approach the Bible with the confidence and nobility of a religion professor I once had. In his opening lecture he said the intellectual goal of the class was to study the Bible scientifically. He confidently asserted that religious bias, church dogma, or Sunday-school learning would not corrupt the sanctity of our scholarly pursuit. His oration was quite persuasive, but throughout the course he violated his own standards, forsaking a scientific approach for his personal dogma. He only proved the point that he, along with all atheists and believers, fundamentalists and liberals, educated and uneducated persons, bring personal bias, individual world-views, and previous learning to every text. Our goal is not to be "bias free," but rather, to enter into a conversation with the text, acknowledging and noting our prejudices, and seek to listen and avoid imposing on the text.[11]

Our previous learning about the Bible is both good and bad. Some of our understanding comes from the writings of literally thousands of men and women who have worked diligently to understand the message of the Bible. Their efforts illumine Scripture and Christian theology. This is good, and the church, society, and our lives are enriched by them. At the same time the sources that help us understand Scripture— a teacher, minister, theologian, or theological system—may become an impediment to further understanding. This paradox is a daily occurrence. Christian communicators subtly refuse to submit our thinking (ego) about the text to a possibly better understanding of the text. We easily fall into the trap of substituting "a system" for the text. Thus, tradition quietly replaces the Bible.

Previous interpretations of Scripture, tradition, biased learning, and the lack of objectivity lead to the problem of manipulating the Bible. The Bible can be manipulated in several ways. First, some use the Bible as a good-luck charm—like a rabbit's foot or four-leaf clover. The Bible, however, is not a "magic book" and will not automatically provoke integrity when used to swear an oath. It is not a truth serum. The power is in the Bible's message.

Second, some Christian communicators use the Bible like a machine gun, firing quote after quote at some perceived objector. Perhaps you have heard messages where biblical quotes are rapidly cited, giving the impression of a confused communicator. (I'll discuss this further in chapter 6.) A string of biblical quotes might "hit" some need in the audience! This method manipulates the text because it neglects to show the wisdom and insight of a particular text. The deluge of quotes (often taken out of context) leaves little time for reflection.

Third, the Bible is used as an answer book by some. Perhaps you've seen publications that list a human concern and then the simplistic biblical solutions. This may be helpful, but may also be manipulative. It is not manipulative to teach what the Bible says about everyday concerns and how they can be transformed biblically. It becomes manipulative when the goal of the message is merely to convey information. When the message stays only on the informational level, it may mean the communicator is afraid to deal with the pain, ambiguities, and failures of life. It is easy to give information and move on. This is subtle manipulation. The impression is given that right information is enough to lead to right living.

Fourth, some Christian communicators substitute a running commentary of a passage for a pertinent message from the passage. The power of contemporary Christian communication is in the connection of a text to the needs of today. The practical value of Scripture is not then but now. Good Bible commentaries stay within the century and culture of the book. Good Christian communication does not. Too much time spent in other centuries will withhold the Bible from today's concerns and confirm the contemporary prejudice of some that the Christian faith cannot withstand modern scrutiny. The communicator manipulates the text if he or she does not allow it to speak to today.

How to Interpret the Bible: Crisscross Interpretation

The importance and manipulation of the Bible has been discussed, as well as the distinct role and task of the contemporary communicator. But how does one interpret the Bible so that its message "connects" today without manipulating the text? This book will not address all the important issues related to biblical interpretation. However, it will emphasize one of the ways Christian communicators may interpret Scripture accurately. Christian communicators can connect with today and minimize manipulation by using "crisscross interpretation." This interpretive method has three foci: interpretation of the Bible, interpretation of culture, and speaking in culturally relevant ways. It begins with the questions, needs, and issues of today. Communicators must be perceptive observers of trends and contemporary life (as will be discussed in chapter 5). We must interpret the Bible with enough sophistication to understand how, where, and what biblical teaching *authentically* connects to contemporary concerns, issues, problems, and questions.

This method is predicated on a willingness to study Scripture and culture, as well as on using an imaginative, plain-speaking, organized method of delivery. It assumes that the communicator will spend enough time to understand the text or biblical perspective so that he or she may cross from the biblical world to the concerns, problems, events, pains, or issues of today.

Crisscross interpretation moves from our world back to the Bible and from the Bible to our world. It means that every message either begins or ends with Scripture, depending on how it is organized. For instance, crisscross communication does not mean that communicators can start without a detailed analysis of a particular text. Quite the contrary. The more diligently a passage is studied utilizing commentaries, Old or New Testament introductions, and Bible dictionaries, the more clearly the text is understood. The better understood, the more profoundly the passage will connect to an analogous contemporary situation. In this case communicators cross *from* the past *to* the present.

A message may be developed the other way as well. Say, for instance, someone wants to address modern stress. Most of the initial study might include problems of modern life— urbanization, two-income families, sickness, death, relationships, racism, sexism, addictions, and unemployment. Once the communicator adequately and accurately interprets cultural stress, he or she "crosses" into the biblical world, seeking biblical perspective about stress. What is most important in crisscross interpretation is focus and movement. The focus is always on contemporary concerns. The starting point may be either then or now, but at some point the two must "crisscross."

From my perspective, crisscross interpretation must be used in every message. If not, listeners will hear the sermon as irrelevant, arcane, and abstract. They will be convinced that God and the church belong in a museum. Likewise, if the biblical perspective is missing from the message, it not only forecloses on the possibility of God's power breaking into our existence, but opens the question of whether the Christian faith offers anything different from talk shows. Talk shows discuss moral, psychological, and social concerns. Why bother getting up on Sunday for something that is omnipresent on television and radio? Face it, Phil, Oprah, and Rush are a lot more interesting than most Christian communicators. This is Raymond's present dilemma with his church. Is God anywhere to be found in the messages? Crisscross interpretation will help communicators avoid losing the message of the Bible or falling into irrelevancy.

The remainder of this chapter will focus on how to interpret and understand a biblical passage in light of what the author meant for the first readers. E. D. Hirsch Jr.'s honesty is helpful. He says that it is impossible to know the intended meaning of a text for certain. This is especially true when the author is dead (like all the human authors of the Bible) since there is no opportunity to dialogue for clarification. It is an understandable mistake to confuse impossibility of certainty with impossibility of understanding.[12] Historical evidence suggests that the meaning of much of the Bible is accessible and understood by large numbers of people from all ethnic, racial, and economic backgrounds. One of the battles of the Reformation was over the right and ability of each person to interpret the Bible for oneself. Of course, some portions of Scripture remain difficult to interpret and understand. Even Peter wrote that some of Paul's writings are ". . . hard to understand" (2 Peter 3:16).

Crisscross interpretation seeks to utilize the voices of Christians past and present, not to determine a certain meaning of a text, but to ascertain consensus regarding an author's intended meaning. It willingly assumes the burden of working through historical, cultural, and grammatical factors on the way toward a consensus of authorial intention.

To clarify crisscross interpretation, let's assume that the meaning of a text is like a stream. We should not spend our life looking for the underground spring that is the source of a stream (i.e., knowing for certain the author's intention for a text). Rather, we seek an interpretation that keeps within the banks of the stream (consensus of authorial intention). The communicator seeks integrity, not omniscience. If our interpretation remains within the banks, it is an adequate, if not exhaustive, interpretation. Crisscross interpretation, like the stream metaphor, has boundaries (banks) but is not preoccupied with absoluteness in understanding. Not all interpretations are equal. Some may spill over the banks on either side and, therefore, be outside the consensus and perhaps manipulate Scripture.

Since church traditions often muzzle, mute, or distort the voice of the authors, the following guidelines will help one to discern authorial intent within "the banks," avoid manipulating Scripture, and utilize church tradition to illumine rather than obfuscate a passage.

Interpret Scripture within its context.

There is an old saying that one may use the Bible to prove any point. Pick a contemporary social, political, religious, or moral concern and Bible verses can be mustered to support both sides. The problem is *not* that Scripture is contradictory. Rather, Scripture taken out of context, or excerpted, may be used to support virtually any idea—Nazism, anti-Semitism, slavery, sexism, or a flat Earth. Perhaps the most serious way to manipulate Scripture is to use it outside its context.

What is important is to realize that every scriptural passage has a larger context. Meaning for *any* passage may only be retrieved from its *larger context*. Interpreting Scripture within its context comes from understanding the purpose of the entire book, understanding the particular genre of literature, noticing where paragraphs end and begin, and taking an account of what precedes and follows the text. Understanding the historical background of both the book and passage is helpful as well.

Consider the cultural background of the text.

The Bible was written within a particular sociocultural situation. Scripture did not arrive directly from some heavenly culture. Rather, Scripture bears the fingerprints, smell, sweat, and struggle of faith communities (like ours!), trying to live their lives. The human issues of geography, weather, economics, customs, language, work, living conditions, and family life come directly from the life situation of the writer. For example, Jesus was born when Quirinius was governor of Syria (Luke 2:2), became a refugee in Egypt due to the pogroms of King Herod (Matthew 2:13-18), was baptized by John the Baptist in the Jordan River (Matthew 3:13), and was executed at Passover at the hands of the Roman procurator Pontius Pilate (Matthew 27:2). Specific people, events, cultures, and worldviews are reflected in the above texts as well as in virtually all texts of Scripture. The importance of understanding culture and historical background cannot be overemphasized. A good interpretation of the text (i.e., staying within the banks) is impossible without it.

"Punt" when necessary.

The football term "punt" means the offensive unit of a football team has failed to accomplish its goal, so it must return the football to the other team. The metaphor suggests that a particular text may be so difficult to interpret that it is best "turned over" to scholars. Communicators may punt because in spite of diligent study they are still uncertain about the author's intent, do not understand the author's use of language or symbols, are unable to ascertain the cultural, contextual, or historical background of the text, or are uncertain about what to say because of the significant cultural gap between then and now. Let's be honest. Sometimes the symbolism of the book of Revelation is difficult to understand. We may not be sure what Paul meant by baptism of the dead (1 Corinthians 15:29). Hebrews 6:1-6 does seem to suggest salvation may be lost. Unless authorial intent and historical and cultural background are clearly known, it may be wise not to speak from such passages: in essence, punt!

Silence is golden.

Christian communicators have the moral obligation to speak on issues addressed in the Bible. We also have the moral obligation to remain silent where Scripture is silent. Many in our society are cynical about biblical teaching because some Christians and church bodies have made outrageous claims about the Bible that, upon close inspection, the Bible itself does not make. For example, the Creation account (Genesis 1-2) is often cited to prove a particular view of when and how the world was created. The problem is that the Genesis Creation account was not intended to state when and how God created the world.

As I write, a congregation in Chicago has claimed that Jesus will return—yesterday. The time came and went with no Jesus. The leaders claimed a further revelation from God. His return has been postponed until a peace accord is signed between the Israeli government and the Palestine Liberation Organization (P.L.O.). Many members are living in the church building waiting for Jesus to take them to heaven. What is surprising is that for two nights this was a leading story on local television news. One station sent a reporter to interview several people about the church's bold prediction. Some thought the members were brainwashed. Most thought the church leadership was "crazy," and the church lost what credibility it had. This may be an isolated incident, but many have made similar predictions. Scripture teaches that Jesus will return to earth some day. Someone may make a prediction that will be correct. But like a broken watch that is "right" twice a day, such a prediction may be attributable to blind luck! Jesus said to those wanting to know when he might return ". . . no one knows, neither the angels of heaven, nor the Son, but only the Father" (Matthew 24:36).

This Chicago church is a striking example of the point. When communicators fail to be silent where Scripture is silent, the damage to the message of Jesus and the church is incalculable. The integrity of the whole Bible is called into question. Cynics, critics of the church, and nonbelievers are given reasons by the church *not* to believe or seriously consider the truth claims of Christianity. Who wants to be associated with a bunch of religious "weirdos"? If they make such confident predictions that are so clearly wrong, why take seriously anything else someone like them says? Refraining from silence may be one of the more egregious examples of a manipulative use of the Bible.

Learn to distinguish between literal language and literal meaning.

I am often asked if I believe the Bible literally. I enjoy answering, "No, I don't! In fact, *no one* believes the Bible literally." The puzzled look on my inquirer's face tells me my answer was unexpected. I mention that biblical authors often used metaphorical language. For example, I hardly think Jesus viewed himself as a literal vine when he said, "I am the true vine" (John 15:1). Rather, referring to a common and important plant from agriculture, Jesus said he is "like" a vine to his followers. As a vine provides sustenance for the plant that enables grapes to ripen, so Jesus provides spiritual strength and sustenance that produces love, joy, and community to all who believe and obey. Is Jesus a vine (literal language)? Absolutely not! Does Jesus provide strength, joy, love, and community to those who believe (literal meaning)? Absolutely! The issue for contemporary Christian communicators is not belief in the literal *language* of the Bible but belief in the literal *meaning* of the Bible. Distinguishing between literal language and meaning does not cause alarm, detract from the importance of the Bible, or lead to a lower view of the inspiration of Scripture. It merely recognizes and takes seriously the language of the Bible. In order to determine literal meaning we must discuss metaphor and hyperbole.

Metaphor

The terms "word pictures," "nonliteral language," and "figurative language" move us into the world of metaphor. A metaphor creates a comparison between two essentially unlike things in order to suggest a likeness between the two. Usually one of the points of comparison is well known to the audience. The link between the like and unlike produced an "Aha!" or "Now I get it!" to the first readers. For example, Jesus said Christians are the "light" of the world (Matthew 5:14). We may understand "light" and Christians, but what meaning is produced by the linkage? Clearly this metaphor should not be understood literally. Christians are not some type of lightbulb or lantern (literal language). Since the literal language fails to provide meaning, we then must think of literal meaning. The metaphor suggests that Christians should do for the world what light does—illumine darkness (darkness being another metaphor, which means life apart from God). The literal meaning is that Christians should illumine and affect a dark, often immoral world in morally constructive ways. The metaphor "light" is not complicated. Any six-year-old singing "This Little Light of Mine" will probably understand the metaphor: Christians should be helpful to others! Light is a metaphor for morally constructive (helpful to others) behavior.

The power of metaphor lies in its tension and limitation. No metaphor is perfect in its comparison. In other words, no metaphor is complete. When Jesus refers to God as Father (Matthew 6:6-9)[13] he is speaking metaphorically. God is not an it, thing, or distant spirit. God certainly is not anyone's biological father. The metaphor suggests that God is loving, caring, nurturing, and relationally like a loving father. Jesus' use of this metaphor clearly emphasizes the relational and loving nature of God. But the metaphor is limited and creates tension. Some theologians remind us that fathers may be abusive and unkind. For many men and women the term "God as Father" creates distance, hostility, and anything but trust. Further, the implied maleness of God reinforces patriarchy in church and society. But the metaphor of God as Father moves us to consider a whole series of questions regarding the attributes of God. How is God Father? Is God Mother? If we switch metaphors and refer to God as Mother, is the problem solved? How is it possible to trust a God identified as your heavenly Father if your earthly father was absent, violent, chemically dependent, sexually abusive, or emotionally capricious? What are the strengths and limitations of this metaphor?

The point and importance of metaphor is clearly demonstrated in the above example. The tension and limitation of metaphor invite probing, reflecting on, and engaging in its meaning. The result is a better understanding of God and the biblical text.

Biblical writers used metaphor for two reasons. First, it helps the reader better understand spiritual realities that no amount of prose could describe. Second, metaphor enabled Scripture writers to speak of the divine in human history and by so doing move from the familiar (our history, culture, world) to the unfamiliar (God) and therefore help bring meaning and understanding—"Aha! Now I get it!"[14]

Hyperbole

Hyperbole is intentional exaggeration or overstatement for impact. Hyperbole is widely used in many cultures. For instance, I read a review of a Chicago play that the critic called "eye-popping." After seeing the show, I still have my sight! Was the critic wrong or perhaps a liar? From my perspective he was neither. He did not intend his words (literal language) to be taken as literally true. Rather, "eye-popping" refers to the way the director used lights, set changes, fog, lively music, and skilled dancing. The hyperbole "eye-popping" was an exaggerated word that accurately described the visual, high-energy nature of the play.

Jesus often used hyperbole. "If your right eye causes you to sin, tear it out . . ." (Matthew 5:29). "If your right hand causes you to sin, cut it off . . ." (Matthew 5:30). "Be perfect . . . as your heavenly Father is perfect" (Matthew 5:48). "It is easier for a camel to go through the eye of a needle than for someone who is rich to enter the kingdom of God" (Mark 10:25).

The question for communicators is how to determine when Jesus used hyperbole. The answer is that the literal fulfillment of his word is either impossible (be perfect as God is) or would not produce the intended ethical effect. It is still possible to lust and steal even if you mutilate yourself. One may be corrupted by materialistic desire as well as by material goods. The conscious exaggeration helps make an important point. Jesus is saying that lust, stealing, and confidence in material possessions are serious moral offenses. He admonishes all of us to take strong measures, if necessary, to live with integrity.

It is important to discern the literal meaning of hyperbole. In his book *When Religion Gets Sick*, pastoral counselor Wayne Oates cites two extreme examples of the inability to understand hyperbole. In a mental health institution he observed a young woman with a missing right hand. The superintendent of the institution told

Oates that she felt God told her to cut off her hand. A guilt-laden man gouged out his eyes in obedience to the Bible. "If thine eye offend, then pluck it out."[15] Certainly the title of the book, *When Religion Gets Sick*, accurately describes the emotional, spiritual, and psychological state of these individuals. However, I wonder how many are plagued by guilt and tyrannized by obligations because no one taught them the difference between literal words and hyperbole.

Understand how to interpret the different types (genres) of biblical literature.

Parables

More than one-third of all the recorded teachings of Jesus are parables. Sallie McFague insists that the parable is the prime genre of Scripture and the central form of Jesus' teaching.[16] A parable is actually an extended metaphor. Sometimes the story is of ordinary people and events. At other times the story is exaggerated. It is both the ordinary and extraordinary that give the parable its power. Rather than saying the kingdom of God is important, Jesus says the kingdom is like finding a treasure (winning the lottery?). It is so joyous that you'd sell everything for it (Matthew 13:44). Rather than lecturing on the question, "Who is my neighbor?" (Luke 10:29), Jesus tells a parable about a mugging. Several clergy persons walked by the dying victim. A Samaritan, however—someone from a despised racial, economic, and religious class—nursed the man back to life at considerable personal expense. Jesus pushes the question back to the inquirer and us: "Which of these . . . was a neighbor to the man . . . ?" (Luke 10:36). The parable disarms, clarifies, and at times infuriates. And the story does not leave us. It forces all hearers to consider his question in light of their experience. In the midst of our reflections, God comes bringing understanding about that which is mysterious, clarifying the spiritual through the mundane, and disrupting the "business as usual" part of our lives.

Parables have a way of communicating meaning depending on where people see themselves in the story. For instance, I am a Baptist minister. In the above parable a priest and a Levite, the ministers of their day, walked by the man, leaving him to die. In light of my experience, this parable is a critique of the insensitivity of clergy like me to the needs of humanity. Despite the best of intentions and the call from God to establish and sustain community, sometimes ministers like me fail to understand "who is my neighbor." The sinner (Samaritan) *did* what *we* ministers talk about. Frankly, this parable makes me uncomfortable. Others would see it differently, depending on their circumstances.

Parables have a way of drawing hearers into the story, then demanding a response. My discomfort is precisely the impact Jesus wanted. As the parable connects to human experience, it has the power to open listeners to the presence of the Kingdom and its values. Christian communicators may retain the impact of the parable through understanding the audience, characters, and general theological framework.

Narratives

While a significant portion of Jesus' teaching is made up of parables, most of the rest is narrative. Stanley Greidanus says the narrative is the central foundational and all-encompassing genre (type) of the Bible.[17] Thomas Long adds that the claim that the Bible is a storybook (i.e., primarily narrative) is not far from the truth. Narratives (stories) are the dominant literary genre choice of biblical writers.[18]

Communicators are faced with an interesting if not unanswerable question: Why did the biblical writers resort so often to story? Why not simply lay out the information in quick and easy prose like an owner's manual?

Robert Alter points out the unique ability of the narrative genre to describe God's working in history. It captures the tension between God's will and plan for humanity and the actual chaos of history. The biblical narratives depict the interplay between God's design and humanity's disorder, between God's providence and humanity's freedom.[19] Narratives tell this story much more effectively than prose. Since God acts in our history, in the midst of the stories of our lives, the narrative becomes a particularly apt literary form with which to capture the divine human encounter and all the tension it evokes.[20]

In the narrative the message is the story. We do not draw "principles" from the story; rather, the narrative is the message. For example, the corrosive effect of riches is dramatically conveyed in the narrative of the man who had it all yet saw something in Jesus that he lacked (Mark 10:17-31). In a touching observation Mark says Jesus loved him (v. 21). However, the reader feels the pain when ". . . he went away grieving" because Jesus told him, ". . . sell what you own, and . . . follow me" (v. 21).

The narrative does not merely transmit information. The story touches the reader. Long says narrative "does something" to the reader by allowing the reader to identify with one of the characters, and by calling the reader to decision.[21] Narrative, like parables, allows individuals to enter into the story through one's own life situation. In the hands of a creative communicator, people enter into a narrative because the biblical stories tell the story of some aspect of our lives.

When speaking from narratives communicators should remember the following:

1. *The goal.* The goal is to organize the message so hearers will experience anew in their life what the text affirmed in its time.

2. *The role of the characters.* Every narrative has at least two characters. Hebrew narratives usually do not develop characteristics. When details are given, they are important.

3. *The plot.* Like a play or television show, all narratives have a plot. There is a beginning, middle, and end. Often there is conflict, tension, and resolution. The plot is the "story line" that allows hearers to identify with and become engaged in the story.

4. *The presence of God.* Generally, the purpose of telling any narrative is to underscore God's presence with God's people. Often the writer wants to remind, inform, and confirm God's presence so the people might celebrate, confess, repent, witness, and be renewed.[22]

Prophecy

When the word "prophecy" is used, the contemporary mind thinks about Nostradamus or some "religious nut" who predicted Jesus would return to earth in 1993. Unfortunately, the prophetic literature of the Bible (17 Old Testament books) and communicators who use it are sometimes associated with people who have made outlandish and wrong predictions. Because of them, the credibility of a responsible communicator speaking from the prophetic books may be questioned.

I, for one, do not want to abandon these books to "cranks." Quite to the contrary, prophetic books may provide the best texts for messages that address how believers should affect the political order or view social issues. Gerhard von Rad notes:

> It was never presumed that the prophet's oracles were addressed to one set of people and one only, and were, thereafter, to be wrapped up in their rolls and deposited among the records. There must have been people who never forgot that a prophet's teaching always remained relevant for a coming day and generation.[23]

When a prophet's speech was considered especially relevant it was written down, preserved in writing for future generations. The task, then, of contemporary Christian communicators is to reclaim the prophecy of the Bible for what it is and avoid "manipulating" it into a road map for the future.

Mickelsen accurately describes the role of a prophet. A prophet was a spokesperson for God who declared God's will to the people.[24] He or she spoke for God *to* the community *about* the community, nearby nations, and the larger world. Prophets declared God's will—past, present, and future—to the people.

Despite my criticism of those who "manipulate" prophecy to say something it doesn't, prophecy does have a future meaning. However, the future aspect of prophecy, whether judgment or salvation, is directed to the present community, meant to influence present behavior. The prophet was not a speculator. Rather, he or she was a *present* change agent. The role of the prophet then was identical to the role of the contemporary communicator now. Both attempt to understand their culture and God's will in order to induce faith and obedience to God.

The prophetic literature of the Bible is like reading someone's mail. It is a portrait of the struggles, fights, conflicts, successes, and failures of individuals and communities as they lived out the faith in their culture. Since communicators are reading someone's mail, we need to understand the cultural and historic situation in which it was received. We share surprisingly similar struggles. This makes prophecy relevant for contemporary messages. The following steps will help contemporary communicators to interpret prophecy with relevancy:

1. Determine the connection between the sociological, cultural, religious, and political situation then and similar situations today. This is the key to making prophecy relevant. The most important theological issue in prophecy is ethics—personal, communal, and social/political. Communicators look for the ethical teaching of prophecy that transcends cultural differences.[25]

2. Try to ascertain for whom the passage was written.

3. If the passage includes prediction, attempt to determine whether it has been fulfilled or not. If the prophecy has not been fulfilled (as some are), resist imposing interpretations that would not have been understood by the author or first hearers. It is permissible to interpret prophecy in terms of equivalents, analogy, and correspondence.[26] In other words, what similar or analogous contemporary situations does this passage address?

Following these tips will safeguard authorial intent, preserve prophetic imagination for our day, and militate against futuristic speculation.[27]

Poetry

Poetry is more than just Psalms. Obadiah, Micah, Nahum, Habakkuk, Zephaniah, Proverbs, Job, and Song of Solomon are poetry. The books of Isaiah, Jeremiah, Hosea, Joel, and Amos are mostly poetry and there is some poetry in Ezekiel.

Like the prophetic literature, biblical poetry is a "gold mine" for contemporary communicators. The chief reason is the brutal honesty of poetry. The authors of biblical poetry communicated emotions and identified with the feelings of people. For example, Psalm 137 was written about those who lived through the Babylonian captivity. Their country was destroyed. They were forced to live in another country, Babylon. In the midst of this captivity under another's domination the psalmist wrote:

By the rivers of Babylon—
   there we sat down and there we wept
   when we remembered Zion.
                    —Psalm 137:1

The reader feels the raw emotions of loss, homesickness, and captivity. The writer goes on describing their agony at the hands of their gloating victors:

For there our captors
   asked us for songs,
and our tormentors asked for mirth, saying,
   "Sing us one of the songs of Zion!"
                    —Psalm 137:3

To interpret the Psalm properly we must use our heart. Living in forced exile, having no assurance of returning home, perhaps witnessing death, privation, and separation from family, the "victors" rubbed their noses into their terrible fate, demanding they sing happy songs from a time when their city and homes were intact and they were free. As the tormentors laughed and mocked, the despair, discontentment, and anger of their captives rose. The psalmist cried out to the Lord for vindication. The psalm ends with the beatitude:

Happy shall they be who take your little ones
   and dash them against the rock!
                    —Psalm 137:9

If we could get past "happy-face, politically correct church behavior," we would see thousands of people who feel this way regarding their job, spouse, and life situation. They would like to "dash against the rock" those whom they perceive as having done them wrong. Barb can relate to the emotions of this passage. She desperately needs messages that address her fears of recurring cancer and the problems of living with a child who has Down syndrome. She feels alone in her pain. She does not feel like dashing anyone on the rocks. Rather, she feels that life has dashed her on the rocks. Biblical poetry gives contemporary communicators the opportunity to deal with the raw edge of all human emotions.

Unlike Western poetry that balances sound, rhyme, and rhythm, biblical poetry balances thought or a rhythm of ideas. This balance is achieved through parallelism or repetition. The feelings of one line are echoed in the second.[28] There are three basic kinds of poetic echoes or parallelism.

1. *Synonymous Parallelism.* The second line expresses the same thought as the first. Again, referring to Psalm 137:3, the first line says, "For there [in Babylon] our captors asked us for songs." The second line echoes the same thought in other words—"and our tormentors asked for mirth, saying, "Sing us one of the songs of Zion!"

2. *Antithetical Parallelism.* The second line expresses a sharp contrast with the first. For example, the first line of Proverbs 14:35 says, "A servant who deals wisely has the king's favor." The second line offers a stark contrast: "But his wrath falls on one who acts shamefully."

3. *Synthetic Parallelism.* The second line complements the first by additional clarification or explanation.[29] The first line of Psalm 115:9 states: "O Israel, trust in the LORD." The second line further explains, "[The Lord] is their help and their shield."

According to Alter, parallelism in all its forms strengthens, empowers, and heightens each of the lines.[30]

When using biblical poetry for contemporary messages communicators should keep the following in mind:

1. Learn as much as possible about the cultural, religious, and political background that gave rise to the poem.

2. Try to determine the setting of the poem. Was the poem written during exile or perhaps during some life-threatening situation?[31]

3. Read, study, and interpret poems through feelings. Feelings often are not reasonable. Don't "kill" the poem by emphasizing reason. Try to imagine why one wishes the death of the captor's children.

4. Note the author's view of God, society, and community.

5. Use imagination. What contemporary experience would provoke individuals to have similar feelings and perspectives?

Epistle literature

Although narratives, poetry, prophecy, and parables are the major literary genres of the Bible, William Doty says that the epistle is the most dominant literary form in the New Testament. Twenty of twenty-seven books of the New Testament are letters and two other books (Acts and Revelation) contain some epistolary material.

Dave Aune helps contemporary communicators interpret Paul's

letters by showing that they consist of three basic elements: ". . . the opening and closing formulas and the central section of the letters, which they bracket."[32] The opening includes a salutation and thanksgiving. Letters conclude with a peace wish, request for prayer, greetings from others, encouragement to greet each other with a holy kiss, and/or a personal greeting from Paul in those letters where a secretary actually did the writing (e.g., 2 Thessalonians 3:17; Romans 16:22).[33]

The central section or body of the letter is the information Paul intended for his readers. This includes autobiographical statements, questions that churches wanted Paul to answer, themes or concerns Paul wanted to address to the church, travel plans, lifestyle, and theological and ethical teaching.[34]

Letters were addressed to real communities with real questions and concerns. Similar to prophetic literature, Romans, Corinthians, and the letters in Revelation (Revelation 2-3) read like someone else's mail. Perhaps the most important task for Christian communicators is to learn why the author wrote the letter and what the church and culture to which it was addressed were like. Once this is done communicators are better able to "connect" a particular text to an analogous contemporary concern.

Biblical Literature Summary

All genres of Scripture are vehicles to communicate the authors' intent. The following chart summarizes in a word or phrase the primary way each genre communicates authorial intent.

Table 4

Genre	Means of Communicating Authorial Intent
metaphor	comparison
hyperbole	exaggeration
parable	extended comparison
narrative	story
prophecy	social situation
poetry	emotions
epistle	church situation

From Genre to Theme

As contemporary communicators interpret Scripture, several common themes from both Testaments consistently recur. Despite cultural, historical, and genre diversity, there is a thematic unity in the Bible. Robert Grant and David Tracy list four themes:

1. God lives and works in history.
2. God chooses a people.
3. God guides these people.
4. God guides their life and work despite rebellion.[35]

Bilezikian adds that the essential themes of the Bible are God, Christ, the Holy Spirit, salvation, the church, and end times.[36]

Mickelsen sees the common biblical themes in terms of the actions of God. These include:

1. The action of God in creation.
2. The action of God with the people of Israel.
3. The action of God in Christ.
4. The action of God with those in Christ (the church).[37]

Communicators are immeasurably helped by understanding the genre or types of biblical literature. Understanding literary genres is indispensable to biblical interpretation and therefore to a clear understanding of major biblical themes. Understanding biblical literature and themes accomplishes part of the crisscross interpretive method. We now move from the biblical world to our world to discover how Christian communicators "connect" biblical teaching (themes) to contemporary concerns.

Message Content and the Search for an Anchor

Despite an extensive church background, Raymond, Barb, and Susan are looking for an anchor. Other seekers are as well. Raymond wonders if there is anything beyond social concerns refracted from a 1960s leftist agenda. Barb seeks an anchor in the chaos of her suffering amid happy-faced Christians who seem to have no problems. Susan wants an anchor to help her with personal decisions. Talk shows and friends merely dispense superficial advice about doing what feels right. That's precisely the problem. Raymond, Barb, and Susan want something more than feelings and opinions. Is there any anchor beyond feelings and thoughts? Happily, Scripture can provide such an anchor.

Chapter 5

Connection: Becoming Relevant

Raymond, Barb, Susan, and millions of other seekers live fast-paced lives. In the last 5 or 6 years most people have been working longer hours. They are tired and emotionally and spiritually depleted. The only messages that will reach seekers are ones that connect to relevant life issues. It is not that seekers are selfish. Rather, most are "running on empty" and look to messages to give them hope, courage, inspiration, or perspective. Communicators must learn the art and skill of connection.

What is connection? Why is connection essential for contemporary communicators? This chapter will identify and discuss four reasons for missed connections in messages. Using the crisscross interpretive method introduced in chapter 4, two means of developing connection will be demonstrated: crossing from text to now and crossing from today's questions and concerns to the biblical text.

Since connection is vital, the chapter considers ways to identify issues that connect. What matters to people today? What is on their minds? What struggles keep them awake at night?

The chapter ends with a discussion of illustrations. Where does one find them? How do contemporary communicators use personal experience to make appropriate connections with listeners?

Connection Defined

Connection is an intentional rhetorical strategy that demonstrates how the teaching of a Scripture text illumines some aspect of contemporary life. Connection is simply human awareness of divine presence. Through the message, God speaks a living word that touches, inspires, assures, or encourages the individual listener. Connection is a two-edged sword; we rejoice at God's presence but also recognize our human limitations.[1] Synonyms for connection include meaning, relevance, application, and take-home value. Connection makes the message interesting and user-friendly. When connection is present, people will say, "The message spoke to me," or "The message was in my face," or "The message touched my heart." Perhaps the best evidence of effective connection is the comment, "It didn't seem like thirty minutes!"

Connection is always explicit and community determined. In other words, the communicator creates contemporary meaning for a specific group rather than a wide audience. One biblical passage can connect in many different ways to address the diverse needs of different communities. For instance, connection in an African American urban setting is different from connection in an African American rural, agricultural setting. Likewise, the same biblical passage could have different connections in white North Shore Chicago churches than white West Virginia churches in a coal-mining community. Connection would also differ from one community to another within the same economic, ethnic, and geographic area. The needs, issues, and concerns of a particular community determine what the connection will be. It is a theological mistake to think "one size fits all" or that only limited connections can emerge from a given text.

It is also a mistake to *assume* that connection occurs automatically. Too many communicators hurl thoughts like seed but fail to define the contemporary issues that "cross" with a biblical text. A cardinal principle of connection is that it must be community determined and specific.

The Importance of Connection

The importance of connection is not to avoid boredom, although a message with good connections will not be boring. Connection is mandated by theological and biblical reasons. Clyde Fant sees the imperative of connection in the incarnation of Jesus.[2] In the incarnation, God spoke to humanity in understandable ways. God spoke in a specific time, place, and culture. God worked so effectively within culture that Jesus was able to say, "Whoever has seen me has seen the Father" (John 14:9). God's will for the world, the content that God desired to convey, "connected" to humanity through Jesus. To accomplish this connection Jesus used the cultural realities of his day to communicate divine will. Paul also, both in his recorded messages (e.g., Acts 17:16-34; 26:2-29) and in his writings, worked from common ground, experience, questions, and perceptions. The acts of God in the incarnation, the life and ministry of Jesus, and the writings of Paul provide theological and biblical precedent for developing connection as we attempt to communicate today.

Craig A. Loscalzo notes that connection enables us as listeners to identify with the message.[3] When identification (connection) takes place, the story of Exodus, Israel, Jesus, or Peter becomes *our* story. And what Jesus did for others, Jesus may do for us.[4] Time, culture, and distance vanish. Rather than taking hearers back to the first century, the ancient story, teaching, or wisdom breaks into *our* lives now. Explicit connection made in the language and thought forms of the listeners gives the message the opportunity and power to challenge contemporary world-views, cultural assumptions, and values.[5]

Poor connection or implicit connection is more a theological failure than rhetorical failure. Poor connection stymies the power of God to work through the message. The opportunity to awaken or affirm faith is forfeited. Further, a steady diet of poorly connected messages has caused thousands to lose their appetite for the church and the Bible, and to view both as purveyors of empty calories.

Reasons for Failing to Connect

Few would argue that connection is important. The real question then is why, despite good intentions, there is such failure. I am persuaded there are four reasons for the failure of contemporary communicators to connect.

Assuming That Connection Has Occurred

To assume that connection has occurred implies two problems. First, the communicator thinks that the message will *automatically* make connection. Second, the speaker visualizes his or her role as that of an artist, naively content to allow listeners to take away whatever they like. These two problems prove that the role of the communicator is misunderstood. The contemporary communicator's role is to interpret *both* Scripture and culture by affirming their unique perspective and relevance for the community. They owe listeners their best effort to demonstrate the specific relevance of a particular biblical teaching. Connection comes from diligence, hard work, and intentional effort, not by happenstance.

Although message development and delivery are creative endeavors, communicators are not artists, nor is the message an art form. Contemporary communicators who aim only vaguely for connection betray their calling. When connection is vague, opaque, or too general, the message is perceived by most listeners as confusing. What was the speaker trying to say? they wonder.

Communicators may assume that their listeners have significant biblical knowledge and great insight into modern life, and therefore use implicit rather than explicit connection. According to Henry Mitchell, this is a mistake. Most people have a difficult time seeing how biblical teaching connects to poverty, meaninglessness, politics, divorce, or drug addiction. Further, listeners look to communicators to connect the Bible to their situation.[6] Connecting is the communicator's responsibility. *If connection is assumed, it probably does not take place.*

Explicit connection is neither authoritarian nor condescending to the listeners. Quite to the contrary, explicit connection creates a dialogical opportunity. Communicators offer their best efforts to interpret text and culture from personal experience and invite listeners to do the same through their own experience.

The Impact of Television

Baby boomers, those born between 1946 and 1964, were the first generation raised with television. This has had a profound impact in virtually every area of life. It certainly presents an additional challenge for Christian communicators.

As early as 1958 broadcast journalist Edward R. Morrow observed that television is "being used to distract, delude, amuse, and insulate us."[7] Three years later, Newton Minow, newly appointed chairperson of the Federal Communications Commission, told the National Association of Broadcasters that its on-screen product was "a vast wasteland." Minow said:

> You will see a procession of game shows, violence, audience participation shows, formula comedies about totally unbelievable families, blood and thunder, mayhem, violence, sadism, murder, Western bad men, Western good men, private eyes, gangsters, more violence, and cartoons.[8]

Among the prime-time shows in 1961 that provoked this analysis were *The Rifleman*, *Father Knows Best*, *Wyatt Earp*, and *Dobie Gillis*!

A recent national study tried to determine whether television was indeed "a vast wasteland" by studying its impact on college students. Some sobering characteristics of television watchers were discovered:

- They expect to be entertained. Serious topics and serious discussions are viewed as boring.
- They are visually oriented. They relate more quickly to pictures than to words.
- They are not attentive to lecture-format presentations, which often lack motion, color, rapid changes, sound effects, visual effects, music, and drama.
- They expect fast solutions and easy answers to complicated problems. TV commercials and soap operas offer easy solutions and easy answers to many major problems facing the characters within only seconds or—at most—minutes.
- They become bored easily, unless information is fragmented and packaged according to the TV formula.
- They dislike history. TV does not deal with the historical facts effectively, nor does the TV generation.
- They dislike reading. Reading demands concentration and imagination. The reader must construct the scenes, sets, and characters—it's hard work, compared to watching TV.
- Most particularly, they seem to resist learning anything foreign: foreign languages, foreign cultures, foreign religions,

or foreign ideas. Most everything about other cultures or
people on TV is negative; hence, what is there to learn?
- They tend to be more passive than active in classroom situations. They do not participate in the process of learning,
nor do they question their professors as often as they
should. After all, TV viewers are not expected to question
their TV sets.
- They like television and entertainment. Television is not demanding. The viewer just sits there and watches.[9]

Although conducted on "twenty-something" college students,
the description may be true of most people who have been raised
with television. If this is the case, the impact of television on the
mind-set of people under fifty is staggering for Christian communicators. In less than one generation an electronic box has turned
millions into bored, ethnocentric people who want simplistic answers to tough problems and dislike reading, history, and anything
abstract. Neil Postman concluded that television has conditioned a
whole generation to value amusement more than substance and
distraction more than analysis and discussion of serious or complex
issues.[10] Another firm conclusion may be drawn. The impact of
television watching on the listener demands that explicit connection
be made by communicators. Television has changed audiences by
robbing them of their critical capacities. Today there is virtually no
chance of communicating to most people under fifty without making many relevant and meaningful connections.

Biblical Ignorance among Church Members

David Buttrick cites the results of a survey of biblical literacy
among members of many denominations. The Lutheran Church
Missouri Synod had the highest score—40 percent! Most Christian
groups strained to average a score slightly better than 20 percent.[11]
This means everyone is failing. No one passes with a score of 40
percent! Tom Long, viewing the whole of American Christendom,
concludes that knowledge of the Bible is at a low ebb.[12]

Remember, Buttrick's survey and Long's observation are about
church members today! Gavin Reid thinks that familiarity with the
Bible and church tradition is quite different now compared to a

century ago. He cites evangelist D. L. Moody as evidence. An evangelist seeks to convert the agnostic and bring prodigal sons and daughters back to God and the church. An analysis of Moody's messages reveals that he did not engage in apologetics or exposition. Rather, he assumed that his listeners *were* already familiar with biblical concepts and doctrine. This assumption, for his time, was correct. Large numbers of converts, whether "blue-collar" Chicagoans or "blue-blood" Cambridge University students, possessed enough Bible knowledge to understand and respond to his messages. Reid believes that the cultural situation and the assumptions Moody made about the level of general biblical understanding were appropriate then but cannot be made today.[13]

What is clear, for whatever reason, is that today the Bible is a closed book, even to most church members. The problem communicators face is widespread biblical ignorance of even the most basic teachings. It is not that biblical teaching and its application to life have been tried and found meaningless. Rather, the Bible is simply being ignored.

The Role of the Communicator

Chapter 3 argues that the plausibility structure of Western society was destroyed by modernity. In this light, the task of the contemporary communicator, using a crisscross interpretive method, must be that of an interpreter of the Bible and of culture. But Lesslie Newbigin presses that the communicator must not only be an interpreter but a missionary as well. The language, thought, and ideas of the Bible may be so foreign to secularized Western culture that contemporary communicators become missionaries in their own culture. Like missionaries attempting to communicate the Christian faith "cross-culturally," contemporary communicators must accept the way understanding is embodied in language. If not, all efforts at communication will be meaningless and ineffective. We must find cultural references (connections) that enable the communication of biblical teaching. When the biblical message is communicated in the language and thought forms of the people, it has the highest probability of connecting with listeners.[14]

We have at least four reasons—a false assumption that connection has occurred, the negative impact of television, biblical ignorance, and a misunderstanding of the communicator's role—that mandate the need for explicit connection in every message. Our culture has drifted too far over the last forty years (let alone from Moody's time) from whatever Christian heritage it once had. We can no longer assume that connection occurs simply because Scripture is proclaimed.

Connection and "Beating People Up"

After teaching seminarians how to communicate the Christian faith, speaking in churches throughout the country, listening to and watching Christian radio and television, and hearing a multitude of messages, I want to call a moratorium on guilt-provoking, negative, "beat up the folks" messages. No matter what church I attend, no matter what its denomination or theology, most messages that I hear are trying to "spank" listeners overtly or subtly. On the theological left I am scolded for voting Republican, for lacking a social conscience, and for noninvolvement in social issues. On the right I am chided for not loving God more, not winning my neighbor to Christ, not attending Sunday evening services, and being too "cozy" with secular humanists and New Agers. Both right and left have consensus in one area: they "beat people up" for not putting enough in the offering plate!

Why do so many communicate such negative messages? There are several reasons. Some copy what they heard during their formative years. Some clergy members are simply frustrated with church life. Some communicators are so cynical that they can hardly make positive comments about anything. For others, messages that "beat up" reflect their theological understanding. They believe that God is mad at everybody and every one of their messages conveys this point. Some project their own unresolved anger and hostility to seekers.

Those who favor "beat up" messages seem to believe that connection comes only through angry, guilt-inducing tones. Somehow, their Good News always sounds bad! Leander Keck refers to such messages as "moralizing." He defines moralizing as drawing moral inferences about things to be done, virtues to be developed, or beliefs to be held.[15] Certainly the Bible speaks about correct beliefs, virtues, and behaviors. James calls for an active, practical faith: "Faith by itself, if it has no works, is dead" (James 2:17). But Keck argues that moralizing, "beat people up" messages actually contradict biblical teaching. They do so in a number of ways.

- They turn the Bible into a codebook.
- They turn Christianity into legalism.
- They make Christian faith too individualistic.
- Perhaps most significantly, they confuse the nature of the indicative and imperative of the gospel. It is only because of the presence of the Kingdom, the indicative, that people have the power, desire, and ability to change and obey the imperative. Since God offers God's self to humanity, the imperative is a gift for the purpose of harmonious relationships among those transformed by God's power.
- Moralizing idealizes the past in ways the Bible does not.
- Moralizing messages miss or scarcely affirm the doctrines of election, the kingdom of God, spiritual gifts, the atonement, and the ministry of the Holy Spirit.[16]

Elizabeth Achtemeier adds that "beat people up" messages fail for two reasons. First, they assume that both communicators and listeners have the power to "get their act together." To the contrary, Scripture assumes that humanity cannot "get its act together." Second, God's actions of grace are shunted to the side.[17] Contemporary communicators must, for the sake of the gospel, world evangelization, and cultural relevancy, stop "beating people up" in their messages!

Mitchell, a longtime observer of the church, addresses this issue. Jesus may have come to comfort the afflicted and afflict the comfortable, but he was not called or paid by them! Negative communicators are not prophetic, priestly, or pastoral. Little they say will empower their hearers. Mitchell pleads with communicators to avoid using messages as whipping posts for hearers.[18]

If life change, integrity, and obedience to the imperative (both personal and social) are important, the surprising truth is that celebrating the goodness of God and the love of God for humanity is the best way to motivate people to obey God's will. The content and connection of a message should make the hearer rejoice.[19] Your grandmother was right when she said, "You catch more flies with honey than with vinegar"!

Connection: From Text to Now

Crisscross interpretation recognizes that connection can move from the text to contemporary questions, concerns, and issues or vice versa. In either case, the message must "cross" to the other world for either connection or content. Greidanus reminds communicators that our goal is not to "make" the Bible connect; it already does. Rather, it is to determine where and how the Bible connects to contemporary realities.[20] Communicators, then, seek an analogy between the situation in a text and a contemporary individual, ecclesiastical, cultural, political, or ecological situation. The key questions are, What does the text say or imply about God's presence in the world (past, present, and future)? and What does the text call Christians to do?[21] In all cases, the goal is to look to the human situation of the text.[22] It is precisely the human dimension that enables connection across time and culture. There are at least six human connections from the "then" of the biblical text to the "now" of our day.

Questions

The Bible is full of questions! What strikes me is both the abundance of questions and the contemporary nature of the questions. For example:
- "What is truth?" (John 18:38)
- Why do you question? (See Mark 2:1-12.)
- What is most important? (See Mark 12:28-34.)
- "Is it lawful for a man to divorce his wife?" (Mark 10:2)
- Is there life after death? (See Mark 12:18-27.)
- "My God, my God, why have you forsaken me?" (Mark 15:34)
- "What must I do to inherit eternal life?" (Mark 10:17)

Admittedly, some biblical answers may not be as comprehensive as we might like. However, the biblical questions and the concomitant perspective on them are relevant and helpful.

Analogous Church Situations

The Bible was written to and for the community of faith. In describing prophetic and epistolary literature "as reading another's mail," I acknowledge the community focus of Scripture. Since people are still people, many analogous situations and problems exist in the contemporary church. Paul writes about conflict—Euodia and Syntyche did not get along (Philippians 4:2)—and misuse of the charismatic gifts (1 Corinthians 12–14). He addresses individuals who are misinformed about Jesus' return (2 Thessalonians 2) and Jewish/Christian relationships (Romans 9-11). Both John and Paul discuss church/state tension (Romans 13:1-7; Revelation 13:1-10). Virtually every passage of Scripture treats some concern of the church or covenant community. Many of these are remarkably similar to present-day church situations and issues.

Analogous Ethical Situations

In the postmodern era, ethics will continue to hold paradoxical roles in society. On one hand, ethical pluralism pervades virtually every area. Western society will continue to drift from whatever ethical consensus it once had. On the other hand, ethics will play an increasingly important role in the management of social institutions. Does anyone believe that Congress, the Supreme Court, business, or state government has the commitment and courage to lead such discussion about ethical issues? In the vacuum created by ethical pluralism, contemporary communicators have a unique opportunity to help shape the ethics of state and social institutions.

Ethical living in every area of life is a major theme of Scripture, beginning with the Ten Commandments (Exodus 20:1-17) and ending with judgment on everyone who loves and practices falsehood (Revelation 22:14). Biblical ethics includes individual, social, political, and ecological morality. Communicators have a rare opportunity to contribute to the moral direction of society by drawing creatively on Scriptural themes and honestly facing contemporary objections with thoughtful explanations.

Western society is paying a heavy price for violating biblical ethics. Sexual freedom now kills. Divorce has created its own industry as psychologists and lawyers try to save those who, in Carley Simon's words, "drown in love's debris." Children of divorced parents experience the loneliness and pain of separation. Some knock on the counselor's door, hoping that therapy will help fill the void created by an absent parent. Millions have lost their lives in war during this century alone because the divine and unqualified "no" about killing was ignored or explained away. Most Americans are cynical about important American institutions. Cynicism has been fueled by disclosure that some leaders have engaged in lying and immoral, self-serving behavior.

Analogous Emotions

Scripture discusses all human emotions: delight, joy, hope, gratitude, affection, love, pride, sympathy, and pity—as well as anger, shame, hate, envy, sorrow, grief, anxiety, and jealousy. Messages on emotions must deal with the psychology of emotions. Fortunately, in recent years much research has been published on love, affection, anger, shame, grief, anxiety, and jealousy. The subject of human emotions is one in which Scripture informs psychology and psychology informs Scripture. Whenever a message deals with human emotions, connection is almost guaranteed.

Analogous Decision or Transition Points

Christian faith calls for many decisions. The communicator should search the text to determine what the text is calling Christians to decide. The connection may be for the individual, the church community, society, or government.

Analogous Life Situations

In any text communicators should look to see what it says about common human experiences and responses. We can find worry, fear, motivations, affections, birth, sickness, love, death, job loss, divorce, relationships, evil, violence, pain, and suffering in Scripture and in life today.

Connection: From Now to the Text

We have considered connections that are made by analyzing the text and then "crossing" from text to now. In this section connection will begin by analyzing today's concerns, questions, issues, and problems and then "crossing" to the text.

Contemporary communicators are faced with important questions: Where are contemporary concerns, questions, and issues addressed? Where do communicators turn to gauge the pulse of American society? If a few selected forums could be located, they could become a resource for message selection, content, and connection. There are many options: best-selling and classic books, books by minority writers, plays, art, television, magazines, and newspapers. However, I am persuaded that talk-show radio and television programs may be the best places to identify critical questions, issues, and trends of our day. Perhaps one reason that talk shows provide this is that the hosts reflect the racial and gender mosaic of America. There are talk shows in Spanish, in German, and with closed captions. There are hosts of every race. There are male hosts, female hosts, left-wing hosts, and right-wing hosts. There are youthful hosts and silver-haired hosts.

I have suggested talk shows as a resource to students, clergy members, professional colleagues, and church members. Their first response is usually ridicule or embarrassment—"I can't believe you said that!" Many disagree, arguing that most talk shows on most days are preoccupied with trite, superficial, sexual, voyeuristic, and sensational subject matter. Some describe them as "teleporn" and "trash TV."[23] These criticisms may be true; yet there are over nineteen nationally syndicated television talk shows. Several important radio stations have moved or are moving to an all-talk format. During the late 1980s many thought that the genre had peaked and saturated the market and would be in decline by the mid-1990s. The opposite is the case.

Ava Thompson Greenwell, assistant professor of Northwestern University's Medill School of Journalism, offers a sociological reason for the rise of talk shows. It is the best forum in the television age to learn what people think and do. "It used to be that people were able to gossip in their own community. But we're more isolated now; we don't know what our neighbors are doing and thinking. These shows give people a window into the world without feeling nosy."[24] This window is exactly what communicators need in the search for connection.

According to Greenwell, the popularity of talk shows is attributable to urbanization. In urban centers, impersonal relationships reduce the sense of community (see chapter 2) that prevails in less-populous areas. Talk shows provide an artificial community where issues of interest are honestly and often sensitively addressed. Sol Feldman, the executive producer of one talk show, says its success is due to populist emphasis. He and the staff seek to learn America's interests, concerns, questions, and pains, then develop shows and find guests that will deal with them.[25]

Many may dismiss talk shows, but the motivated communicator realizes that anything that so profoundly connects must be studied. An analysis of the content and method of talk shows yields two important lessons for contemporary communicators.

First, even though television has reduced the scope of interests of typical Americans, they will still listen far longer than the average sermon lasts if *their* needs, interests, and concerns are addressed. This lesson is actually frightening. It may suggest that many contemporary Christian communicators are answering unasked questions or addressing passé subjects. Could it be that talk shows have indicted gospel communicators? Could it be that Christian communicators select only a few human concerns and, by neglecting the rest, unwittingly encourage people to bury their feelings, struggles, and temptations? Could it be that *our* messages are trite, superficial, and egocentric? Perhaps some talk shows are "trash TV," but perhaps just as many "trash messages" come from the pulpit.

Cheryl Jarvis lists the four top-rated, nationally syndicated talk shows from Chicago. Their hosts are Jenny Jones, Oprah Winfrey, Jerry Springer, and Bertice Berry.[26] Their topics have included weight loss, high school violence, neglected children, and parenting. Three of the four shows have discussed child raising and the breakdown of family and community. Even the subject of Oprah Winfrey's weight loss actually dealt with women's self-esteem, confidence, and hope. If these samples of the highest-rated shows reflect people's concerns, questions, and problems, I would argue that all are biblical subjects. Obviously, talk shows do not deal with these issues in biblical perspective. However, they provide communicators with concerns that do need to be addressed from the biblical perspective.

Second, extensive research goes into discovering what people are thinking and what the content of shows should be. It is estimated that there are only two hundred topics in the entire repertoire of *all* talk shows. Yet it is not unusual for talk-show producers and staff members to review three hundred publications per week looking for a new idea, a new story, or a new twist on an old story. Talk shows connect because they have people who study, evaluate, and try to understand those they want to reach.

Contemporary communicators do not have the time, money, or staff to emulate talk-show research efforts. The challenge is to practice personal diligence in the effort to understand people we want to reach. Contemporary communicators must not dismiss talk shows as pornographic, voyeuristic, or superficial. Rather, we must look to discover the fundamental human concern behind the medium and then address it in biblical perspective.

Illustrations

Throughout the centuries Christian communicators have used illustrations to bring understanding. Illustrations are shared experiences, perspectives, or stories that illumine the text. They help clarify abstractions.[27]

Illustrations are particularly important to contemporary communicators in light of the general lack of Bible knowledge. To communicate biblical content effectively today, more rather than fewer stories and illustrations are needed. Communicators should be aware of eight guidelines when choosing and using illustrations.

Keep illustrations under control.

The key question is, Does a story facilitate identification with some important aspect of the message? Occasionally a student will deliver a message in one of my classes and tell a great story that has no perceivable connection to the message. When class members offer feedback, I frequently ask why the story was used. After a few furtive glances and some shuffling feet, the student usually says, "But it was such a great story, I had to tell it." Students are not alone. Many veteran speakers do this too. However, to be effective, every illustration must directly link to the message.

Keep all stories/illustrations short.

If stories are too long or complicated they last longer than listeners do.

Resist the temptation to use "illustration books."

Many of these books have been around for decades. After reading and even using them, I have serious questions about the integrity of the stories and accompanying "documentation." If there is a question about a story's veracity and plausibility, it is better not to use it, no matter how well it would fit!

These books often quote famous Christians from previous generations. Few people today know or care about what Spurgeon said, Luther did, or Calvin wrote. Their contributions are important. However, they should be highlighted in other teaching opportunities, not in contemporary messages.

Don't claim another's experience as your own.

Doing this is unethical. Instead, say, "A friend of mine . . ." or "In her book, author 'X' said how she felt when . . ." or "This week on 'Nightline' Ted Koppel interviewed 'X.' I was taken aback when he said . . ."

Communicate effectively with humor.

It is appropriate to use humor if it helps to clarify some aspect of the message. Some wonder if humor is suitable during worship in view of the solemnity of the occasion. They fear that it might ruin the decorum of worship. Each congregation must decide this issue for itself. However, from a contemporary perspective, most seekers perceive worship as boring, partly because of what seems to be phony solemnity and seriousness. Appropriate humor may help break this unnatural barrier so that more culturally appropriate worship may occur. Humor enlivens worship and helps the communicator to connect.

One caution should be mentioned. Often comedic humor is characterized by the use of subtle and/or overt insults. Much of this humor centers on sexuality, ethnicity, gender, or tragic life events. As funny as it may be, put-down humor, except when directed at oneself, should be avoided for practical and theological reasons. Put-down humor works against the message, creating discomfort rather than encouragement. It also sets a socially destructive example.

Be careful about using illustrations from the lives of others.

This is especially true if you are a pastor. The traveling speaker should observe this for ethical reasons, but the pastor needs to be cautious for both ethical and practical ones. If the pastor's illustrations come from the life of the local church, even if veiled, one's integrity is compromised. Why should I trust someone who may use my story as an illustration next Sunday? However, people's stories may be used with their permission. The communicator might say, "Jim and Rita Smith, members of our church, said I could tell . . ."

Get the story right!

Whenever you use a story or illustration, make sure the facts are correct. This is another issue of integrity. If the dates, story line, or characters are incorrect, the communicator loses credibility with those who know the facts. Seekers are knowledgeable!

Create illustrations from your personal experience and perspective.

But when you use your experience, O. C. Edwards says, "you're damned if you do and damned if you don't." Divulge too much of your personal perceptions and feelings, and you run the risk of being perceived as self-absorbed and overexposed. On the other hand, the communicator who is never autobiographical seems aloof, distant, and out-of-touch.[28]

So the question is, How does one share one's pain and experience and maintain balance? This is an important question since so much public speaking has been at extremes. Some speakers leave the impression they are above the struggles they talk about. They become stuffy purveyors of biblical information. In contrast, other speakers engage in talk-show confession. They become host and guest; desires, pain, and experiences are shared in inappropriate ways.

Despite the extremes of others, contemporary communicators should understand the importance of personal disclosure but also recognize the need for boundaries. Communicators do have the right to privacy. As positive as I am about the way talk shows define important questions, concerns, and issues, one unfortunate side effect is the "tell-all" expectations that carry over to the church. Communicators have no obligation to pander to these expectations. But how does one cull from one's life and struggles yet maintain boundaries?

One technique is to collectivize human experience. Most communicators will admit we've experienced significant difficulties, if we're honest with ourselves. But some of these difficulties may be too personal and still hurt too much. Yet this pain brings credibility, authenticity, and depth to our speaking. If we collectivize it we can use our pain and experience but with less personal risk. For instance, suppose your teenage son got drunk at the prom last night and was carried home by his friends in a wheelbarrow. To make matters worse, this Sunday's message is on parenting. It would betray family loyalties to say, "Sometimes teenage sons drive parents nuts. This week I got so mad at my son when he got drunk at the prom." It might be appropriate to say, "Sometimes it's tough parenting teenagers, as some of us know. But sometimes it's tougher being a teenager and living with parents who don't seem to get it, like many of us remember."

I once heard a speaker describe his problem with lust. He assured us that he could identify with our struggles in this area. There was little doubt that he could, but he embarrassed himself and his audience with the details. His laudable goal of identification about this sensitive subject failed. It could have succeeded if he had collectivized his experiences. He might have said something to this effect: "Most of us struggle with our sexuality. We affirm fidelity but often are tempted. We can identify with the sentiments expressed in the hymn that says, 'Prone to wander, Lord, I feel it' and the popular song that tells us we should love the one we're with." By collectivizing experience, speakers can be warm, creative, and vulnerable but maintain balanced boundaries. They can draw from personal issues but inspire listeners to reflect on their own. Identification and boundaries are both established.

There is an additional advantage to collectivizing human experience: it fosters a dialogue between speaker and audience. If I merely talk about my experience, sin, and story, you remain a listener. If I invite you to remember a similar story from your experience, I am in dialogue with you. This creates connection.

Not every experience, pain, or struggle has to be collectivized, but there are three areas in which collectivism is wise: family life, past and present relationships with the opposite sex, and current church relationships (if one is on a church staff).

In an ideal world, communicators could be more vulnerable. Perhaps Christian groups should be able to deal with sensitive issues so honestly and openly that collectivism would be unnecessary. However, this is not yet the case. Disclosing too much about one's sexuality, family, and past relationships in the present climate of American society increases the risk of misinterpretation and misunderstanding. Speakers must find personal comfort levels while noting the above problems, their ministry context, their temperament, and their personal and family sensitivities.

Finding Connection through One's Experience

Empirical data underscores the value of one's experience as a source of connection. Steven Van Ostran studied effective communicators in midsized churches. He discovered that these ministers placed a high value on integrating illustrations, stories, and anecdotes with their own lives. In other words, all stories and illustrations had a personal dimension for the speaker even if they were collectivized or adapted.[29] But how does one use experience as a tool to build connection with people? Four disciplines provide speakers with resources.

Read

In a small city, a new seminary graduate in her first church wanted to continue her education by enrolling in a Ph.D. program at a nearby university. When the church budget was being formulated, she requested a tuition allowance. The church leaders seemed agreeable, but she worried whether the congregation would support such a budget item because it had never been done before. Also, she was a young pastor and most of the members were older. None had college degrees. The business meeting came and the congregation voted on her pay package, including an amount for her Ph.D. Everything passed unanimously, and the church supported her educational goals and wished her success.

Happily surprised, the pastor asked an older member why things went so smoothly. He said, "Your predecessor's messages got pretty thin. We think he quit reading. We don't want that to happen to you."

This story clearly shows the importance of reading, both for message content and connection. Reading keeps one awake to cultural realities. The church has historically valued reading and educated ministers. Churches started colleges and universities for the purpose of creating a "literate clergy," or as the founders of Harvard College said, because they were afraid ". . . to leave to the churches an illiterate clergy when our present ministers lie in the dust." The church has been less concerned about credentials than educating ministers who are able to think, speak, read, and write. The church, then and now, views reading as an important value that keeps communicators in touch with important issues of our day. If messages are "thin," it is probably due to lack of reading and study!

Communicators must read widely, especially in the areas of sociology, psychology, history, and current events. At the same time they must study the Bible, theology, and church history. Scripture has a way of putting a moral mirror before our face, culture, and church life. Church history gives perspective on how other generations of Christians wrestled with problems similar to the ones we face. Minimum reading materials include leading newspapers, a weekly news magazine, and Christian periodicals from different theological perspectives. Newspaper editorials are particularly helpful because they discuss significant issues often overlooked by talk shows.

Observe

On a rainy, cold day I conducted a funeral for an elderly Christian. In another corner of the cemetery I saw balloons, streamers, and birthday banners. It was so unusual that I detoured to the colorful display. Gifts, cards, pictures, and candy decorated the grave of a boy named Ryan who would have been four years old that day. Apparently a few hours before, his family had had a birthday party for him at his grave. I knelt, read the cards, and wept for a child I didn't know. I wish I had been there earlier to cry with the family.

The next week was Easter. I ended my Easter message with Ryan's story and what Easter means for Ryan, his family, and all who mourn. Jesus wept for all who are broken by life's realities. But in the midst of the brokenness, which even Jesus experienced, he offers hope for our lives and world.

Many speakers refuse to observe what is happening in society because they fear contamination. Observation does not mean agreement. But observation will lead to the understanding and empathy so vital for effective communication. Look. Observe. You will discover real, useful resources all around you.

Listen

In many ways reading and observing are synonymous with listening. But reading and observing are more comprehensive, while listening is more specific and personal. Ministers have the "best seat in the house" when it comes to listening to individuals. Most people welcome those who initiate conversation about their personal well-being. A simple phone call to say, "I hear things are tough. Let's have lunch," is often *still* warmly welcomed. No matter how large a church or ministry, some time every week should be spent listening to individual struggles, pains, and concerns. Collectivization begins with listening to people.

Listening one-on-one is not the only way to listen. We have already discussed the opportunities that talk radio and television offer.

Feel

Some communicators are primarily thinkers; others feel. All struggle with balance since contemporary messages must engage both thought and feeling. One of the gifts a communicator can give listeners is to feel with them the pain of living. Communicators feel the problem of divorce, not in statistics but in the eyes of the man whose children are with his ex-wife this weekend. They feel the problem of loneliness in the pain of the widow, isolated because her husband and friends have died. They sense the problem of health care, not in political debate but in a mother who refuses to see a physician herself so that her children will have what they need.

If contemporary communicators can read, observe, listen, and feel, they will likely connect with people's questions, problems, hurts, and desires in their messages. When this is done, even those of limited ability will be acclaimed geniuses.[30] But more importantly, communicators will bring the grace and presence of God to daily life.

Connection: The Search for Relevance

If seekers evaluated messages like Olympic ice-skating judges, there would only be one criterion—connection. "Tens" would only be given to messages with immediate connection, application, or take-home value. Connection addresses everyday down-home life issues such as Raymond's quest for community and God, Barb's struggle with cancer, and Susan's personal and ethical dilemmas. Seekers are looking for help for immediate concerns. They don't want a genius, just someone with "guts" who will let the light of biblical content shine on their concerns, pains, and questions.

Chapter 6

Organization: Transforming Ideas into a Message

Why organize? A seed-hurling communicator may believe that organization stifles lively messages, but the connection-building communicator finds message organization indispensable. What can message organization do for one's effectiveness as a speaker? How does one begin to organize a message? Although there are many methods of organization, this chapter presents a specific method—one that has the advantage of being sensitive to the contemporary cultural realities of oral communication and the needs of seekers.

The Need for Effective Message Organization

Frequently I offer a money-back tuition guarantee on the first day of class. I guarantee that *if* students do what is taught, they will improve their ability to communicate the Christian faith by 100 percent. This approach is meant to capture attention, but it is also a serious offer. I want to motivate students to work hard. I also want them to expect improvement in their ability to communicate. Those who are intentional about message organization *will* become better communicators.

In communication or homiletics theory the terms "form," "structure," "construct," "build," "develop," and "arrange" are often used to describe the process of creating a message. I prefer the term "organization." This describes more precisely the specific strategic decisions that create the flow, development, and movement of a message. All communicators engage in some form of message organization. Good organization transforms raw information into a message.

The importance of organization for Christian communicators cannot be overemphasized. Researchers from Dynamic Communications International surveyed hundreds of people immediately after they listened to a message. As many as three out of four (75 percent) had no idea what was communicated.[1] James Daane likens the message organization of most evangelical pastors to shoddy building construction. He says that messages are often built so poorly that they would collapse if they were physical structures.[2] Haddon Robinson believes that most listeners leave church services not hearing a message but ". . . a basketful of fragments with no adequate sense of the whole."[3]

In contemporary American church life and other forums where efforts are made to communicate the Christian faith, well-organized messages are the exception rather than the rule. With improved organization, Christian communicators can develop effective, even exceptional, messages.

The Importance of Message Organization

Message organization is vital for at least four reasons. The first reason is the *human brain*. Neurological studies of brain function suggest that sensory data is not taken in by the brain as an undifferentiated mass. Rather, the brain engages in selective perception and discrimination. Information is abstracted, grouped, and shaped by the brain. The mind finds and imposes connections.[4] Hence, the brain itself works to organize data. Mitchell believes that the mind is not receptive to messages that make little sense and have no discernible organization.[5] Therefore, good message organization works in cooperation with brain functioning to help listeners experience and understand the message's content.

The second reason is *communication theory*. Communication theory distinguishes between thinking about a particular subject and trying to communicate about it. What seems clear to the speaker may not be clear to the listeners. Communication is a process that involves entering the world of others and in some way trying to affect them.[6] Communicators cannot assume that what they intend to say is understood as intended. Listener perception, personality, and culture influence how a message is experienced. The speaker's subject, vocabulary, and attitude also determine how listeners understand the message. Disorganized messages complicate the communication process by creating confusion between communicator and listener.

The third reason is *the Bible*. The Bible, the content and anchor of contemporary Christian communication, is largely unknown in secularized Western society. Chapter 3 discussed the fact that modernity has dismantled the Christian plausibility structure of Western society. The residue of the Christian plausibility structure appears quaint, irrelevant, boring, or meaningless to large (and increasing) segments of the West. This phenomenon creates "zero tolerance" for confusing, boring, and irrelevant messages.

In the past, dull messages got reinforcement from an underlying Christian plausibility structure. That day is long gone! Dull messages receive no reinforcement from the social order. Instead they collapse. Church and parachurch groups now bear sole responsibility outside the home for the Christian faith and teaching. Christian communicators face a different opportunity and burden than did our predecessors. In order to meet this cultural challenge, messages must be relevant and clear to listeners. Relevance and clarity require the firm foundation of organization.

The fourth reason is *faith*. This may be the most important reason for sound message organization. Fred Craddock argues that message organization shapes listeners' experience of the Bible passage from which the message came, which in turn shapes their faith.[7] And isn't the shaping of faith the purpose of every Christian communicator?

Basic Considerations of Message Organization

Four basic considerations set the stage for message organization. First, one must accept the burden for it. While some claim that organization is unnecessary, arguing that the experience of the listener determines meaning, I contend otherwise. Well-organized messages increase the likelihood of a listener's meaningful experience. Therefore, communicators must organize the message in a way that maximizes understanding, clarity, relevance, and meaning for the listener.

The need to connect with one's audience mandates message organization. Assuming the burden of organization is the contemporary communicator's first step toward accomplishing effective communication. Success or failure lies in the communicator's hands, not the listeners' hands.

Second, there is no one best organizational scheme. Don Wardlaw has long advocated finding clues in the Scripture text for organizing the message. We also know that different genres of Scripture suggest different ways to organize messages.[8]

Third, the attention span of Americans should be noted. The average American can concentrate about four minutes per idea. This means that twenty-five-minute messages can have only five or six distinct ideas. Since all messages need a beginning and ending, the time remaining permits only three to four ideas, moves, or points.[9]

Fourth, message organization helps the communicator narrow the message. Reuel L. Howe and the faculty of the Institute for Advanced Pastoral Studies once researched the frustration that both ministers and listeners experience with preaching. Listeners almost unanimously complained that messages contained too many ideas and were not relevant to contemporary needs.[10] Howe doesn't describe the scope of the messages' content. Was it sufficiently narrowed, or were the messages wide-ranging? In either case, there were too many ideas with too little linkage. Howe's research adds to the argument for better message organization as a way to facilitate connection with contemporary listeners.

A Contemporary Method of Message Organization

From a contemporary perspective, message organization consists of making two strategic decisions and then taking six action steps. The term "strategy" suggests the intentional activities of organizing a message. Strategy means the development of a plan of action that leads to a desired end. For our purposes, strategic decision one (see table 5) is determining "what" the communicator wants to say. To complete strategic decision one, three action steps—(a) determining a subject, (b) writing a message statement, and (c) articulating a goal—must be accomplished.

Strategic decision two (table 5) is establishing "how" to unfold for listeners the "what" of strategic decision one. The three action steps within the "how" include: (a) determining the most appropriate move pattern, (b) developing the beginning, and (c) developing the ending.

Table 5

Message Organization

I. Strategic Decision One: What?

    Action Steps:

    A. Determine the subject.

    B. Write the message statement.

    C. Articulate the goal.

II. Strategic Decision Two: How?

    Action Steps:

    A. Determine the most appropriate move pattern.

    B. Develop the beginning.

    C. Develop the ending.

Strategic Decision One: The "What" of the Message

Chapter 4 defined the role of contemporary communicators as interpreters of culture and the Bible. They utilize the crisscross interpretive method, looking for connection between biblical teaching and current questions, issues, and events. As I write, America is transfixed with the O. J. Simpson tragedy. A great athlete and celebrity stands accused of killing his former wife and another person. We wonder how such a "nice guy" could be accused of such a heinous deed. Scripture has much to say about character, the human potential for evil, appearance in contrast with reality, and the importance of justice. Polls about Simpson's guilt or innocence find that whites are certain he is guilty while African Americans think the case is less certain than it appears. Many African Americans remember how the justice system has been used to thwart justice. The Simpson case points to the continuing problem of racism in America. This story, as well as many others that are less sensational, raises questions, issues, and concerns that Scripture has already addressed.

At some point, perhaps every weekend if one is a pastor, the communicator must begin to organize what he or she is going to say. How does one begin? If, for instance, the communicator decides to speak about human nature in light of the O. J. Simpson case, the story itself suggests appropriate texts. One crosses from today to the text. If the communicator starts with a text, he or she should look to those issues and concerns in the text that listeners care about and that easily "cross" to our world.[11] Once the communicator crosses *from* the text or *to* the text and has identified a connection between the text and listeners, the first step of message organization has been made. The subject of the message is developing.

Step 1: Determine the Subject.

A subject is a one- or two-word statement that tells what the message is about. One or two words may seem inadequate, but in reality they serve to narrow what will be said. How does one state the subject of a message? Picture a gathering of friends in a restaurant after church. Another friend who overslept and missed the service joins them and asks what the morning message was about. The one- or two-word response identifies the subject of the message!

The subject answers the question, What is the message about? The subject must be developed from the listeners' perspective. It must be interesting and relevant, address an important contemporary need, and be of personal concern to the listeners.[12] Possible subjects that spring from the O. J. Simpson case are domestic violence, anger, image, accountability, self-awareness, jealousy, justice, and racism. Texts could be "'. . . all who take the sword will perish by the sword'" (Matthew 26:52); ". . . do not let the sun go down on your anger . . ." (Ephesians 4:26); ". . . take the log out of your own eye . . ." (Matthew 7:5); and "'Let anyone among you who is without sin be the first to throw a stone . . .'"

(John 8:7). Each provides somber warnings about violence, uncontrolled anger, and blindness to one's own hypocrisy.

Let us assume that back at the restaurant no one at the table could say in one or two words what the message was about. This means that the message was probably confusing, vague, unconnected, or unclear.

Step 2: Write a Message Statement.

Although determining the subject helps to narrow what will be said, a still sharper focus is needed. The next step, writing a message statement, brings the sharp focus. The subject is general; the message statement is specific and addresses a particular aspect of the subject. It delimits the subject. A message statement is the one central idea, theme, or experience to be communicated in the message. This statement brings the text and contemporary human concerns together in a six-to-eight-word affirmative statement.

Three issues pertain to message statements. First, there is only one message statement per message. Two or three ideas in a message statement will be perceived by listeners as two or three messages. Vague message statements result in confused listeners.

Second, what I call the message statement others call the central idea, big idea, thesis statement, theme statement, purpose statement, proposition, or subject sentence. Although each term may have a different shade of meaning, they all function the same way. Whether the terms are from rhetoric, homiletics, or communication theory, they cry out in unison that an effective message communicates only one specific idea or experience.

Third, the struggle necessary for writing a message statement may be the hardest—but most important—part of message organization. Without a strong message statement most messages drift at sea. If the message were a building, the message statement would be the foundation, the support for the entire message. Gerhard Hauser warns communicators that Americans are inundated with information. The result is that many people dread receiving excessive information.[13] A well-crafted message statement is a sensitive way to deal with this pervasive cultural reality. It is friendly to listeners.

Craddock articulates three reasons for the importance of a message statement. First, it *gives focus to the message* and increases the likelihood that the speaker will connect with seekers and not merely hurl seeds. Second, it *gives confidence to both the speaker and listeners*. Seekers have confidence in speakers who provide a steady diet of well-organized messages. Why? Because experience has taught them that when these communicators invite them on a journey, together they will go somewhere. They won't simply wander in the woods. Third, a good message statement *enhances creativity and imagination*. Creativity among musicians and actors blossoms when they know their music or lines. Creativity is released precisely because it is bounded and controlled. Likewise, creativity and imagination will be most evident in well-organized messages.

The message statement functions in the same capacity as a bouncer for a bar. Let's assume that a group of collegians decide to go to the local watering hole. As they approach a popular hangout in their college town, they find a muscular, no-nonsense person standing in the middle of the doorway checking identifications. He is the bouncer. He inspects their driver's licenses and permits them to enter if they have appropriate credentials. The bouncer has done his job when those who are underage are turned away.

For our purposes the message statement is the "bouncer" for the entire message. It determines what should be included and it throws out unsuitable ideas and experiences—anything that shows up without proper credentials.

The more focused the message statement, the better it will "bounce out" extraneous material. In the end, the message will have a high probability of being relevant, important, and worthy of listeners' attention.

Step 3: Articulate a Goal for the Message.

A goal is a desired result. Goals state what the communicator wants seekers to be, become, understand, feel, or do. The goal of a message clarifies the desired behavioral effect or attitudinal change in the lives of seekers. Impact, effect, purpose, intent, and aim are synonyms for goal.

Many Christian communicators have difficulty articulating what they want their message to accomplish. From a rhetorical and theological perspective all messages have a purpose or goal. Theologically, the proclamation of the gospel has a definite goal. The message of the prophets, Jesus, and the apostles was never, "Let me throw out a few ideas." Rather, it was and is, "'The time is fulfilled, and the kingdom of God has come near; repent, and believe in the good news'" (Mark 1:15). Clearly, each of them had a goal in view!

Rhetorically, a message is always directed to a specific group of seekers with a specific goal in mind for them. The message or speech anticipates that seekers will accept the particular point of view of the message or speech and act on it.[14]

Some may think that a goal-oriented message is manipulative. Any message can be organized in a manipulative way, but messages should be persuasive rather than manipulative. Contemporary communicators seek to persuade seekers that the truth claims of Christianity are superior to the claims of all rivals. At the same time, Christian communicators must respect seekers by leaving space for them to accept, reject, or dialogue about Christian truth claims.

Christian communicators do not pretend to be value free. They honestly admit their persuasive intention. Manipulation does not occur because they have a goal to persuade. Rather, they manipulate if they do not allow seekers the choice to reject the message with seeker self-esteem intact!

There can be many message goals, depending on the subject, message statement, and needs of listeners. For example, a message could be planned to inform, teach, persuade, encourage, share experience, motivate, inspire, and/or incite action. If the goal is to inform or teach, seekers should think in new or different ways as a result of the message. If the goal is to persuade or motivate, seekers should act. If the goal is to share experience, seekers should identify with some character in the text. If the goal is inspiration and encouragement, seekers should experience hope, self-esteem, or a greater awareness of God's love. The essence of a message goal is appropriately targeting the message to the heart (emotions), the mind (reason), and the will (volition) of the seeker. From the many possible goals, every message should have only one clear goal.

Table 6

Message Goals and Results

Goal	Results
Persuade	Action
Share Experience	Indentification
Encourage	Sense of hope, self-esteem

Good message goals have three characteristics. First, there is coherence between the goal and the subject and message statement. For example, if the subject is human nature and the message statement is "All people are capable of doing evil," then the goal should not be "to recruit twenty volunteers for the soup kitchen." A more appropriate and coherent goal would be to "help people acknowledge their own tendencies toward violence" or to "give courage to seek counseling for domestic violence."

Second, the goal must be articulated with a specific group in mind. Every message is given to a specific group.[15] Therefore, four questions should be asked of the subject and message statement. These questions will help the communicator articulate a goal for the specific audience.

1. What do seekers know about the subject?

2. What do seekers believe about the subject?

3. What prejudices do seekers have about the subject?

4. How do I organize the message that intersects with seeker experience?[16]

The more information the communicator has about seeker knowledge, beliefs, and prejudices, the better a message goal that intersects with seeker experience can be articulated.

Hauser adds another dimension. The message goal should not only be influenced by listeners' knowledge, beliefs, prejudices, and experience but also by their interest in the subject and their willingness to change. The following table, adapted for seekers, suggests how interest and openness to change may be used to write an appropriate goal for the message. By answering the four questions above and using table 7, the contemporary communicator may more precisely articulate a message goal with a high probability of making a significant impact on seekers.

Table 7

Seeker Interest in Subject	Seeker Openness to Change	Appropriate Message Goal
1. High interest in subject	High openness to change	Target message goal to change behavior and/or attitude.
2. Low interest in subject	High openness to change	Target message goal to kindle interest in subject.
3. High interest in subject	Low openness to change	Target message goal to future and/or deal with listener impediments to change.
4. Low interest	Low openness	Communication is futile.

Source: Gerhard A. Hauser, *Introduction to Rhetorical Theory*

A personal example may clarify how the above process is both practical and helpful. A few days after the state of Illinois executed John Wayne Gacy, one of the world's most egregious mass murderers, I gave a message on capital punishment. Strategic decision one, the "what" of the message, looked like this:

Subject:	Capital Punishment.
Message Statement:	Capital punishment is an immoral method of justice.
Message Goal:	To change people's perceptions on the justice of capital punishment.

I determined that my listeners were interested in the subject and open to change, but viewed capital punishment as just and biblically permissible in certain cases. However, after the message was delivered, I discovered more about my audience. I was right about their interest in the subject, but wrong about their willingness to change. My message failed because I wanted to persuade listeners intellectually that capital punishment was biblically immoral, even for someone like Gacy. While I articulated arguments, my listeners identified with the victims and their families. Gacy was convicted by overwhelming evidence of killing thirty-three young men. Most of the bodies were found buried in Gacy's home, not far from the church. My failure to understand listeners' grief and pain led me to an inappropriate and ineffective message goal. When I talked about justice, the listeners heard me asking for compassion for Gacy. Listeners wanted justice for the victims and their families, not Gacy.

Listeners' interest; openness to change; and knowledge, beliefs, prejudices, and experience with the subject should not determine the content of the message, only the message goal. Had I been more aware of listeners' beliefs, prejudices, and lack of openness to change I could have articulated a more appropriate goal or waited several months before speaking on the subject. The message failed, not because of content, but because I articulated an inappropriate goal. There was high interest but low openness to change.

Strategic decision one of message organization (subject, message statement, and goal) functions like the skeletal system of the body. In the healthy body, bones don't call attention to themselves. They actually are noticed when they are missing or covered with too little flesh. They should be present but not visible. Similarly, strategic decision one should not call attention to itself. Rather, it should quietly control what is said, understood, and experienced.

The practical question of whether or not the communicator should reveal his or her working message statement and goal gets its answer from the type of goal the speaker has (strategic decision two). At times the message statement may be stated. If the goal of the message is to inform or teach, then the message statement should be included early in the talk. If the goal is to encourage, motivate, or share experience, then the message statement fits well just before the ending. What is important is that the communicator has the freedom to reveal the message statement or not, as suits the message.

Strategic Decision Two: The "How" of the Message

Strategic decision one must precede strategic decision two. "What" precedes "how." When strategic decision one is accomplished, the communicator has an embryonic message and then may begin to work on its organization.

Just as three steps compose strategic decision one, the "what" of message organization, three steps also occur in strategic decision two, the "how" of message organization. These steps include (a) designing the move pattern; (b) writing the beginning; and (c) writing the ending (see table 5).

Step 1: Design the Move Pattern.

The move pattern of a message is the coherent development and elaboration of the message statement. Most of the content of the message is within the move pattern. Buttrick uses the term "move" to describe what others call the body or points of the speech or message. Whether this step is called the body, points, main ideas, or major and minor premises, it includes two to four major concepts, shifts in direction, or points that are linked coherently to the message statement.[17] The term "move pattern" describes well the coherent flow of the message. Like a river, the message flows in a determined design and within the "banks" of its aim. The move pattern facilitates the communication of the message statement and goal. Just as there are many subjects, message statements, and goals, there are several move patterns. We will consider seven.

The Narrative Pattern

This pattern is like a three-act play. Typically, act one reveals a particular situation, problem, or issue; act two intensifies the problem; and act three brings illumination, resolution, or perspective to the problem or issue.[18]

This pattern has the advantage of preserving the story quality of narratives. The message statement links listeners with one of the characters in the narrative. The goal is to have listeners experience in their life what one of the characters experienced in the narrative.

When this pattern is used, the communicator must rigorously follow the three steps of strategic decision one, since a biblical narrative includes many problems, issues, or places with potential for identification. A narrative pattern is effective if the goal is inspiration, encouragement, or experiential identification.

The Problem-centered Move Pattern

This pattern is helpful when the subject is an important problem or concern of the twentieth century. The following example utilizes the problem-centered move pattern for the text John 14:6. The steps of strategic decision one are:

Subject:	Salvation.
Message Statement:	Jesus is the only way to God.
Message Goal:	To persuade listeners to respond to Jesus in faith.

The beginning then sets up the problem. One way to begin would be:

> We've got a real and embarrassing problem. We can either evade it, ignore it, pretend it doesn't exist, or simply turn the page. Who wants to listen to a narrow-minded know-it-all? The world is full of them. An answer for every problem! Who needs them? Jesus sounds like those street-corner preachers! He's got the truth and knows the way! Maybe Jesus should be dismissed as quickly as most dismiss street preachers. Both make outrageous claims, right?

The move pattern suggests options that listeners have when considering Jesus' narrow claim. The last move could present the possibility that Jesus' claims might be true. Another variation of this pattern is to state the problem, analyze it, and either suggest a solution or offer some biblical perspective on it.[19]

The advantage of this pattern is the unique way in which it can be sensitive to important and controversial twentieth-century issues and concerns and at the same time be in conversation with Scripture.

The weakness of this pattern is that it can be used to distort Scripture or to promise more than Scripture actually promises.

The Ideal/Actual Pattern

In Luke 4:16-21 Jesus announces what his ministry will accomplish. In him the long-awaited Kingdom is dawning. Those in bondage will be freed. The sick and blind will be healed. Most seekers today would understand Jesus' rhetoric as mere campaign promises. There is a significant gap between Jesus' promises and reality. What happened?

The steps of strategic decision one for a message on this text using an ideal/actual pattern might be:

Subject:	The Kingdom.
Message Statement:	In Jesus the Kingdom comes to our community.
Message Goal:	To awaken believers to the power of the Kingdom.

The ideal/actual pattern for this message would involve two moves. First, the communicator would discuss the power of the Kingdom for the community—the ideal. Second, he or she would discuss where the Kingdom is to be found in the midst of suffering, pain, and evil. The strength of this move pattern is its ability to address contemporary concerns, like suffering and hypocrisy, in light of biblical teaching. It holds in tension God's promises and the painful realities of life. Both the ideal and actual may honestly be explored.

A Teaching Move Pattern

In Luke 9:18-27 Jesus asks his disciples a straightforward question: Who am I? To those seekers (most of America, according to many polls) the question is still *relevant*. The steps of strategic decision one might be:

Subject:	Jesus' Identity.
Message Statement:	Jesus introduces himself to our generation.
Message Goal:	To teach seekers who Jesus is to our generation.

The move pattern would expand and explain Jesus' identity in
light of the text. The advantage of this move pattern is its ability to
articulate to our contemporary culture significant didactic (teaching) material in the Bible.

The Question/Answer Pattern

In Mark 10:17-22 a person "runs up" to Jesus and asks, "What
must I do to inherit eternal life?" This age-old question is
relevant to every generation. Modern medicine, good nutrition,
and aerobics may have postponed but not slain "the last enemy
. . . death" (1 Corinthians 15:26). The steps of strategic decision
one might be:

Subject:	Eternal Life.
Message Statement:	Jesus gives eternal life to all who believe.
Message Goal:	To answer the question, How does one attain eternal life through faith in Jesus?

The move pattern would pose the question, supply answers from
other religions and ideologies, and then articulate the Christian
perspective. The steps could be slightly rearranged so that the goal
would be a decision. If the goal of the message is to inform,
persuade, or deal with contemporary or biblical questions, then this
is an effective move pattern.

Not This/But That Pattern

In John 8:31-36 Jesus declares that true freedom comes by
believing and obeying him. This statement is incredible to modern
ears. Freedom is having the ability, opportunity, and courage to do
what one wants. Slavery, not freedom, is obeying someone else.
The near obsession with personal freedom in Western society and
the vastly different understanding Jesus has on the subject makes
this another relevant subject. The steps of strategic decision one
might be:

Subject:	True Freedom.
Message Statement:	Jesus offers true freedom to humanity.
Message Goal:	To persuade listeners that freedom comes through faith and obedience.

A three-shift move pattern could work like this:
1. Freedom is *not* choosing your own values.
2. Freedom is *not* trying to please others.
3. Freedom *is* believing and obeying Jesus.

If the goal is to inform, persuade, teach, or deal with contemporary misperceptions on some aspect of the Christian faith, this is an effective move pattern.

Ambiguity-to-Clarity Pattern

Angels are enjoying a resurgence of popularity. I counted nine books on angels in a suburban Chicago bookstore. Angels have been the topic of several talk shows. Although angels are often mentioned throughout both testaments of the Bible, few Christians know much about them. If a Christian communicator wanted to clarify ideas about angels, the steps of strategic decision one could be:

Subject:	Angels.
Message Statement:	Angels exist.
Message Goal:	To inform listeners about what the Bible teaches about angels.

The move pattern would have two shifts: First, discuss the ambiguous role of angels both in Scripture and contemporary understanding. Second, using biblical texts and modern personal experiences, explain the role of angels in the contemporary world.

This move pattern is effective when the subject is vague, ambiguous, or sounds unbelievable to modern ears. By acknowledging ambiguity, clarity on the subject is achieved. Table 8 summarizes move patterns and message goals.

Table 8
Move Patterns and Message Goals

Move Pattern	Message Goal
1. Narrative	Experience, Inspire, Encourage
2. Problem Centered	Teach, Persuade, Apologetic
3. Ideal/Actual	Motivate, Apologetic
4. Teaching	Teach, Apologetic, Decision

5. Question/Answer	Teach, Inform, Decision, Apologetic
6. Not This/But That	Teach, Apologetic, Decision
7. Ambiguity to Clarity	Teach, Apologetic, Decision

Step 2: Develop the Beginning.

Within the first seconds, seekers ask themselves a series of questions that determine whether they will continue to listen or daydream during a message. Is the speaker credible? Does the speaker know what he or she is talking about? Is the subject interesting? These assessments are made quickly, so the old adage, "You don't have a second shot to make a first impression," is particularly true for Christian communicators. An effective beginning, then, may well determine whether or not listeners will hear anything else in the message.

Mike Hostetler maintains that the beginning must relate to the subject and be relevant to the listener at the same time.[20] To do this the communicator must connect the subject to a seeker's interest, concern, or experience. This may be accomplished through a story, quotation, observation, current event, question, or statistical study.

One of the more effective ways to open a message is to create tension regarding the subject. For example, let's assume that the subject is God's concern for people. A beginning that creates tension regarding God's concern for people might be: "Most of us are familiar with this chorus: 'God is so good, God is so good, God is so good, God's so good to me.' Do you think the people starving in Rwanda or those forced into prostitution in Southeast Asia or those dying of AIDS sing this song? Are we kidding ourselves, or may only rich and fortunate Christians join the song?"

This opening relates to listeners in several ways. First, it speaks of God's care while acknowledging tension between God's care and human suffering. Second, by creating tension between God's care and human suffering, it invites listeners to reflect on their own suffering in light of God's concern for them. Further, it signals to listeners that the speaker is open, honest, aware, and approachable. She or he takes people seriously enough to deal honestly with their pain.

Good beginnings build rapport and interest and set up the subject with listeners. Beginnings that are friendly, low-key, and positive are favorably received by listeners.[21]

There is some debate on the best length for a good beginning. Robinson advocates twenty-five to fifty words;[22] Ferris Whitesell believes that the beginning should be between 5 percent and 15 percent of the total time of the message.[23] Hostetler says the beginning should be about 20 percent of the total message time, or five minutes of a twenty-five-minute message. He adds that a more complicated subject usually requires a longer beginning.[24]

Step 3: Develop the Ending.

The ending is the last move of the message, and its purpose is to complete the message. J. Alfred Smith likens the ending to landing an airplane. The pilot directs the aircraft to its intended destination according to a flight plan. The communicator brings the message to its ending, determined by the goal of the message.[25] The message must be "landed," not left "circling" the listeners.

There are at least six different types of endings. No new ideas should be presented in the ending.

1. *The Summary Ending:* The message statement and moves are simply restated.

2. *The Illustration Ending:* The message concludes with a story. The story must be consistent with the message statement and goal and be so clear that there is little need for interpretive or explanatory comments. The story or illustration must make the point.

3. *Question Ending:* The message ends with a question or series of questions. The question rises up and gives voice to those already being asked by listeners.

4. *Quote Ending:* The message ends with a quotation. As with illustration endings, aptness and clarity are essential. The quote cannot be bland or susceptible to multiple interpretations. It must link with the subject, message statement, goal, and move pattern.

5. *Celebrative Ending:* The message statement and move pattern

lead to an ending of joy, praise, and celebration. The ending celebrates the goodness of God's love and actions that give hope for our lives and world.[26]

6. *Decision Ending:* The ending calls listeners to respond to the message statement according to the message goal. Decision endings could elicit praise, faith, joy, gladness, renewed dedication to Kingdom values, or ethical resolve.

Transitions

Thus far I have argued that message organization consists of two strategic decisions—"what" and "how" (table 5). "What" includes (a) determining the subject, (b) writing the message statement, and (c) articulating the goal. "How" involves (a) planning the beginning, (b) selecting one of the seven move patterns, and then (c) developing one of the six types of endings.

Table 9

Message Organization

BEGINNING

Transition

FIRST MOVE
Transition
SECOND MOVE
Transition
THIRD MOVE

Transition

ENDING

Since the beginning and ending are moves, the move pattern itself should contain no more than four moves or shifts. As the communicator proceeds from the beginning to the first move of the move pattern, or from one move to the next, or from the last move of the move pattern to the ending, listeners need help. Table 9 diagrams what should occur. A consistent problem is that what seems clear to the speaker leaves seekers confused. Either the move pattern blends into one confused heap or there is no discernible link between one move and the next, thus leaving a gap. Listeners feel they've heard six different messages rather than one message with a well-planned move pattern. Effective use of transitions helps to improve the flow from one idea to the next.

Transitions are the bridges between the moves of the message. They close off *and* also clearly link the ideas within the message. There should be a transition between the beginning and the first move of the move pattern, between each move of the move pattern, and between the last move of the move pattern and the ending. Transitions, like bridges, keep moves distinct yet make possible the progression from one to the next.

Effective transitions may be sentences, clauses, or well-placed pauses (silence). Some possible transitions are:

"That's the first reason, but there is a second one. . . ."

"That's the bad news. Now, the good news. . . ."

"That was then, but now . . ."

"But that's not all. . . ."

"I hear what you are thinking. . . ."

"I hear that stuff too, but here is how I experience it. . . ."

"Although I understand, I am still puzzled. . . ."

"On the one hand . . . but on the other . . ."

When the communicator has completed strategic decisions one and two as well as climbed the six steps, the message is ready to be communicated.

Organization: The Search for Clarity

The Bible as the anchor and content for Christian communication to seekers is an easy argument to make. The importance of connection and relevance using the Bible is easy as well. If you take Scripture seriously and use crisscross interpretation, it really will be quite hard to bore seekers. Scripture speaks to their most pressing questions, concerns, and pains.

The case for message organization is a little harder to make. Seekers will never say that a message was poorly organized. But when seekers are confused by what was said or how it connects to their lives, often the culprit is poor organization. The speaker was not clear in his or her own mind regarding strategic issue one: the subject, message statement, and goal. Therefore, biblical content and connection tripped at the organizational starting line and failed before a word was ever uttered. Seekers demand clarity of thought and delivery. They simply will not listen to someone who rambles with little direction. Good message organization, then, not only transforms ideas into messages; it may also help transform the seekers themselves through the spoken word.

Chapter 7

Authenticity: Speaking with Passion, Heart, and Soul

This chapter presents insights from rhetoric, communication theory, psychology, and theater that focus on the integrity of the communicator.

An important question should be raised: Is the Christian communicator helped or hindered by these insights? Perhaps Christian communication is such a different "animal" from other types of oral communication that the use of secular knowledge and methods will destroy or corrupt the message. Christian communication is different—very different from other types of oral communication. Most importantly, the content and ethics of the Christian message are already determined and cannot be changed. The unalterable message is the Bible (see chapter 4), not church tradition. Woe to the communicator who alters biblical content. The curse of adding or subtracting from the Bible's teaching (Revelation 22:18,19) is intended for contemporary communicators as well as it was for the first hearers of the book of Revelation! Postmodern culture presents to communicators established patterns, biases, questions, and expectations that largely determine how individuals will hear, understand, and respond to the Christian message and biblical teaching. Speakers must acknowledge these givens and work with them.

Those who are serious about communicating to seekers start first with their needs, questions, issues, and concerns. Therefore, any insights from communication, psychology, theater, rhetoric, or other sources that help establish the Christian message or understand modern culture or seekers are most welcome. Rather than fearing insights, contemporary communicators should embrace all ideas on how to articulate more effectively the gospel, as long as the message is not compromised.

How Do You Speak to Seekers?

There is a simple answer to the often-asked question, What is the best way to deliver a message to seekers? The one and only answer is, *Your way!*[1] In other words, speaking involves all of one's being. All speakers bring our own personality, emotions, world-view, and pain to our messages. This in turn influences how we use our voice, eyes, and body. Personality, experience, and world-view also shape how speakers view Scripture and seekers. In addition, speakers do not merely deliver a message. Rather, our voice, body, and face work to nonverbally communicate our personality.[2] We are part of the message. One's "heart and soul" or lack of "heart and soul" is always evident.

This chapter explores the psychological dimension of communication (i.e., how the inner world of the speaker shapes the message), the link between words and body, and how speakers can develop "your way" messages. Two elements are essential for "your way" messages to seekers: activating one's emotional memory[3] and using one's eyes, voice, and body congruent with one's emotional memory.

What's Emotional Memory?

By definition, emotional memory is the ability of the speaker to engage in and deeply experience the feelings, suffering, and joy of the text and subject of the message. Most human emotions are experienced by age eighteen.[4] All speakers have a reservoir from which to draw. Using crisscross interpretation (see chapter 4), the speaker looks for how and where the text crosses to contemporary human concerns. In study and reflection, the text and emerging subject bring the speaker in touch with personal feelings, pains, joys, hopes, and fears. Therefore, emotional memory is the appropriate use of one's experience, including one's joys, sorrows, sadness, failures, hopes, pain, anger, rage, elation, successes, and fears, past and present, as they relate to the text and subject.

Activating one's emotional memory is the first step toward connection (see chapter 5). If a text or subject does not connect with the speaker's emotional memory, there is little hope that the message will be more than a discourse on first-century religious thought. If a text or subject "connects" with the speaker's emotional memory, it likely will connect with seekers as well.

Chapter 5, on connection, suggests that reading, observing, listening, and feeling are ways to find connection. All are activities that help activate one's emotional memory.

I remind you of a distinction between emotional memory and experience. Emotional memory is one's life experience of the more distant past. Experience describes current or more recent encounters. In either case, the Scripture or subject "triggers" analogous emotions or experiences. When this "triggering" occurs, a double connection is produced. First, there is a genuine and personal revelation from the text to the speaker. Second, the speaker is then able to articulate with relevancy and meaning the importance of the text and subject to listeners. Why? Emotional memory brings together the text, the subject of the message, and the lives of both speaker and listener. This encounter leads to relevance and intimacy.

Some think that the communicator ought somehow to get out of the way of the message. They say that the use of one's emotional memory and experience is precisely the problem of contemporary preaching. What is needed in our narcissistic culture, some argue, is less human involvement and more attention to divine truth claims. *More* biblical information is needed with *less* "heart, soul, and emotional memory." If this is done, God is more glorified and the Bible more honored. In this view, the speaker is merely a channel, vessel, or instrument for God's use. The less present and visible, the better.

Contemporary communicators must reject this impersonal and mechanical view of Christian communication. We must recognize that we are part of a message. The message is not a collection of abstract biblical ideas disembodied from the communicator. Rather, the message is embodied in the communicator. It is therefore a biblical and theological mistake to reduce the human dimension of communication. God's glory and honor are not in competition with the human dimension of communication. Rather, God works through our humanness and engages all aspects of our being. The speaker is not a channel, vessel, or instrument for a message but *becomes* the message through the power of God working through Scripture, human personality, emotional memory, and experiences. By God's design the human dimension of proclaiming the Good News brings glory, honor, and praise to God. Anyone can simply read the Bible and make a few comments. But when the speaker's emotional memory is engaged in the service of the text, he or she is a witness to the transforming power of God and the possibilities of God for seekers. Minimizing this human dimension actually minimizes God's glory. The Bible delegates ministry and communicating the Christian faith to human beings. Jesus gave the apostles and the church the task of proclaiming the presence of the Kingdom until "the end of the age." Paul adds that the message of the cross (Romans 10:14-15) is communicated by human speakers. If Jesus and Paul elevate the human dimension of proclamation and ministry, I remain puzzled why some seek to minimize it.

For contemporary communicators, Jesus and Paul prove the importance of the human dimension of speaking. Others have also emphasized this. Aristotle said that the personal character of the speaker is the most important component of an effective speech. Speakers perceived as having good character are believed more fully and readily by listeners.[5] Centuries later, Phillips Brooks highlighted the same theme. He defined preaching as communicating truth through personality.[6] For Brooks, this meant that the character, emotions, will, thoughts, and feelings of the speaker should be on display in every message. There simply is no room for impersonal, mechanical, or "infomercial" preaching.

Sigmund Freud in *General Introduction to Psycho-Analysis* adds that words call forth emotions in both speakers and listeners.[7] A strong consensus emerges from psychotherapy, rhetoric, and homiletics on the bond between emotions and words. Words cannot (and should not) be devoid of authentic emotions. Rather, one's emotional memory provides words with power (Freud), personality (Brooks), and character (Aristotle). The speaker's words will "connect" with listeners when words and emotions are congruent. In other words, when one speaks from one's emotional memory, one will connect with and be perceived as authentic by seekers.

Congruence Between Emotional Memory and Words: How?

How does one attain congruence between one's emotional memory and experience and the words of a message? The answer depends on how one views the role of the speaker. Should the speaker stand apart, distant, aloof, and dispassionate from the message? Or should a speaker stand inside and within the message? The answer to these questions is essential. If one agrees with the first option, messages will be more objective and less emotional. However, the speaker will be perceived by seekers as a college professor, actor, news reporter, or travel guide in an ancient land. If the speaker does *not* stand inside the message and is *not* emotionally engaged, seekers will perceive him or her as detached and artificial.

I am persuaded that contemporary Christian communicators must stand inside the message. This means that we are part of the message, constantly using our emotional memory to connect the text to ourselves and to listeners. Further, seekers expect speakers to be part of their message. In other words, they want to feel, see, and hear the "heart, passion, and soul" of the communicator. As mentioned, there is a direct correlation between the presence of emotional memory and the believability of the message. Why? To use a contemporary phrase, the message is perceived as "coming from the heart," and therefore is worth believing.

Congruency between words and emotional memory is not achieved by mastering certain rhetorical techniques, faking the proper emotions, or trying to "work up" the suitable emotion. At best, these methods will be effective if the speaker is a good actor, speaks infrequently, or gives the same message to different audiences. Rather, the solution is to allow the text to shape one's emotions (i.e., stand inside the message). This is done by trying to find oneself in the text and subject by listening to and allowing it to illumine one's emotional memory.[8] In other words, as one listens to the text, reflects on it and the emerging subject, relevant feelings, memories, and perspectives are recalled by Scripture from one's own life experiences. As the text works on the speaker's emotional memory, it also enables the speaker to hear the analogous painful cries of others.[9]

Table10

How to Use One's Emotional Memory

1. Increase self-awareness.
2. Listen to the human dimensions of Scripture.
3. Feel the pain in the Scripture and analogous pain of others.
4. Invest one's emotions in the message.

Source: Richard Ward, *Speaking from the Heart*

Using one's emotional memory and experience is, frankly, scary. It dredges up past pain and failures, brings to light the "muck and mire" of life that many would prefer to hide, and confronts us with it. It also leads to a question. If contemporary communicators utilize their emotional memory, could it not lead to subjective, egocentric, titillating messages? I have already talked about some of this in chapter 5. The answer to the question is that yes, it's possible, but there is no choice. All speakers will bring some aspect of their emotional memory and experience to their messages. The only question is whether it will be intentional or unintentional, authentic or inauthentic. The most dishonest speaker says, "I am only telling you what the Bible says." This is not only dishonest but hypocritical. No one is bias free. All must admit that our feelings influence how we interpret and understand the text. But as I pointed out in chapter 4, the Bible, not one's feelings, is *the* content of Christian communication. The use of crisscross interpretation and emotional memory may actually mitigate subjectivism. Crisscross interpretation seeks to interpret Scripture authentically for today. Emotional memory is "triggered" and disciplined through the efforts of interpretation. Both seek an authentic and contemporary understanding of Scripture for today. The advantage of crisscross interpretation, using one's emotional memory, and good organization is that the result is "your way" messages. The speaker is able to find genuine voice, passion, heart, and soul that are not muted by past church tradition.

When I was a boy, I watched a show that was locally produced in Cleveland. I don't remember its name, but one of the main characters was Captain Penny. He dressed like an old railroad engineer and ended every show with the same words. Looking into the camera, he said, "Remember boys and girls, you can fool all the people *some* of the time, some of the people *all* of the time, but you can't fool Mom." Captain Penny's aphorism applies to contemporary communicators as well. If we are not ourselves, if contemporary speakers do not utilize emotional memory to develop "your way" messages, we are actually "faking it" by hiding behind someone else. We are engaged in a rhetorical sham. Certainly we will be able to "fool" some and perhaps all of the people "some of the time." But as time passes and relationships develop in community, like Mom, the people can't be fooled with the mask of an inauthentic, incongruent speaking style. The long-term benefit of being oneself, utilizing one's emotional memory, and developing "your way" messages is congruence between words and emotions. You will not have to remake yourself. You become an authentic communicator when what you *say* is who you are. Your messages will have heart, soul, and passion.

Emotional Memory and Authenticity

An even more serious problem than merely fooling someone exists. When words don't match emotions, seekers perceive the speaker as a phony. The speaker's moral integrity is questioned by those whom the communicator seeks to persuade. As Aristotle and Paul remind us, speakers who lack moral integrity produce little moral persuasion.

If there is "zero tolerance" for boring messages today, there is even less tolerance for speakers perceived as phonies. Seekers think communicators are phony when we imitate others (try to fool people), feign humility, use religious jargon, or live hypocritically.

Everyone imitates someone. We learn through imitation. I remember trying to imitate Roberto Clemente's batting stance to improve my hitting and Wilt Chamberlain's method of shooting foul shots to improve my free-throw percentage. (Neither helped.) There is a difference, however, between imitating someone to help discover "your way" (whether hitting, shooting, or speaking) and trying to "fake it" through imitation. Imitation carries with it the possibility of never finding how to speak "your way," heart-and-soul messages. The use of one's emotional memory is particularly important here. It is the best way to avoid imitation, to develop authentic "your way" messages, and to speak with heart, passion, and soul.

Humility is an important biblical value. It recognizes the glory and power of God in the midst of our human limitations. The way humility is often defined and lived out in many church circles has little to do with biblical teaching on humility and much to do with church culture, tradition, and expectations. The problem comes when a communicator affects humility based on church expectations. He or she conforms to church expectations on humility for "points" rather than practicing biblical humility. Since church culture defines this virtue, many conform to these human definitions. This is easy for those whose personality naturally fits church expectations. However, it becomes a problem when a person tries to become humble in a way that does not fit his or her personality. Seekers, more so than believers, intuitively recognize this phony piety for what it is—manipulation. Contemporary communicators should value humility, the kind that is consistent with biblical teaching and *our* personality. However, "one size does not fit all," so we must choose genuineness over insincere conformity.

The use of religious jargon is insensitive to those not familiar with church tradition, language, and symbols. Unlike Jesus, who used everyday populist language to communicate, religious jargon has the effect of obscuring the message by using the language of the "inside crowd." Seekers then dismiss speakers as phonies or irrelevant. A refusal to speak in everyday language reinforces the pervasive prejudice that Christians can't "cut it" in the marketplace and must retreat to our church culture, cliques, rituals, and language.

Nothing turns off seekers and believers more than communicators who do not "practice what we preach." All contemporary communicators are human beings subject to pains, sin, hypocrisy, anger, joy, and frustration. Seekers do not expect perfect consistency. In many ways they are more compassionate and understanding of human peccadillos than the churched. What seekers expect is openness and honesty with the speakers' own struggles and pain in living the Christian life. The air of being above the struggles and immune to everyday temptation and sin both sets communicators up for a fall and breeds cynicism among seekers. When speakers imitate others, feign humility, use religious jargon, and live hypocritically, we are conspiring to fool listeners. But remember: "You can't fool all the people all the time." Most importantly, you can't fool God! Table 11 summarizes phony communication techniques.

Table 11

Phony Communication Techniques

1. Imitating others.
2. Practicing false humility.
3. Using religious jargon.
4. Living hypocritically.

Emotional Memory from the Inside Out

It would be particularly fruitful if we somehow could study the emotional memory of contemporary communicators. This, however, is an impossible task. No generic emotional memory exists. Memory is always specific and varied, so no two communicators have the same emotional memory. This provides each communicator with a unique and creative opportunity to develop "your way," heart-and-soul messages. There is some data, however, on how one's emotional memory and experience influences the message.

Myron Chartier sees a correlation between self-esteem and emotional memory, which in turn shapes the content and connection of messages. Chartier argues that the self-esteem of the communicator is an important dynamic in what (content and connection) and how he or she communicates. It is part of every emotional response, desire, value, goal, and self-perception. Self-esteem influences how the communicator views God, others, and the community. Chartier divides communicators into three groups: low self-esteemers, middle self-esteemers, and high self-esteemers.[10]

Low self-esteemers tend to be self-haters who feel inferior and unlovable. They often project their self-hatred to others. They view life as meaningless. Their messages tend to emphasize a rejecting, unloving, and vindictive God. There is little room for grace.

Middle self-esteemers are self-doubters and reformers. Grace rarely enters their vocabulary or messages and, more importantly, their life. Unsure of themselves, they strive for approval, awards, and success. Their ambition is never satisfied. Messages from this group are likely to be "workaholic" in tone, not to appease an angry God but to accomplish important goals.

High self-esteemers are self-affirmers who feel good and confident about themselves. They are generally affirming people and have a positive view of God and life. Hope is characteristic of their life and messages. Their messages affirm a loving, accepting, and caring God. The Christian faith is joy and celebration.

What is important from Chartier's classification is how the presence or absence of self-esteem influences emotional memory and one's view of God, others, and the world. Self-esteem influences the content and connection of the message. Further, it affects the use of body, voice, and eyes in delivery. In the next chapter we will discuss the use of the body in communicating the gospel to seekers.

Chapter 8

Get Physical! Let Your Body Talk

Carole Channing makes an insightful observation about acting in general and about her award-winning portrayal of Dolly in the play *Hello, Dolly*. She says actors tell the story of their role through their face, voice, and body.[1] Likewise, Christian communicators tell *the* story through their faces, voices, and bodies. Speaking and acting are somatic experiences. A recent book on preaching underscores this practical but all too overlooked fact. Pamela Moeller, like Channing, reminds Christian communicators that preaching is an exercise in bodily movement. In biblical perspective, movement is part of every aspect of life. God creates; the Holy Spirit hovers over creation; and when God speaks, things happen. In our living God there is movement![2]

The act of speaking is an experience of movement. As one speaks, eyes blink, the heart beats, and lungs breathe. Vibration is produced, and the shoulders, arms, and chest cavity move.

Research on effective and ineffective speakers supports the importance of appropriate bodily movement in communication. Allen H. Monroe discovered six characteristics of an ineffective speaker: monotonous voice, stiffness, lack of eye contact, fidgeting, lack of enthusiasm, and weak voice. Conversely, five characteristics of an effective speaker are: direct eye contact, alertness, enthusiasm, pleasant voice, and physical activity.[3] Tables 12 and 13 summarize Monroe's findings.

Table 12

Characteristics of Ineffective Speaking

1. Monotonous voice
2. Stiffness
3. Lack of eye contact
4. Fidgeting
5. Lack of enthusiasm
6. Weak voice

Source: Allen H. Monroe in *Public Speaking: An Audience-Centered Approach*

Table 13

Characteristics of Effective Speaking

1. Direct eye contact
2. Alertness
3. Enthusiasm
4. Pleasant voice
5. Physical activity

Source: Allen H. Monroe in *Public Speaking: An Audience-Centered Approach*

Monroe's research suggests that the difference between effective and ineffective speakers is almost exclusively in the ways individuals use their eyes (face), bodies, and voices. The stiffness and fidgeting of ineffective speakers contrasts with the alertness and enthusiasm of effective ones. The contrast suggests that effective speakers are more emotionally engaged and communicate with verbal and nonverbal congruence.

But Monroe's research identifies a troubling concern. None of the characteristics of effective or ineffective speakers deals with the content of the message. Message quality is based almost totally on the quality of delivery. Message content hardly matters!

Psychologist Albert Mehrabian demonstrated that nonverbal behavior in a speech has more impact in communicating feelings or attitudes to listeners than words. He says that only 7 percent of the emotional impact of a message is communicated by words; 38 percent is communicated by voice inflection, intensity, and loudness;

and 55 percent is communicated through facial expressions.[4] The face and body are significantly more important in communicating emotions than words.

For Christian communicators, this does not mean that messages must immediately become more emotional and gesture filled. Rather, it presents a twofold challenge. First, communicating the gospel should involve the whole body. Second, the use of the eyes, body, and voice is at least as important (more important, based on the above research) as what is said.

The title of this chapter is "Get Physical! Let your Body Talk," an adaptation for Christian communicators from Olivia Newton John's popular song "Let's Get Physical." Although the context of her song and this book are quite different, there is one similarity: our bodies will "talk"! The only question is whether they will talk effectively or ineffectively. Wardlaw is clear about this. Effective messages are characterized by congruence between what is said and how the message is delivered. If there is incongruence between the emotions; content; and use of body, voice, and eyes, the message will not only be ineffective but listeners will perceive the communicator as someone they can't trust. Likewise, congruence between content, emotion, voice, eyes, and body builds trust between the communicator and listener.[5] Words, emotion, voice, eyes, and body must work together for dynamic oral communication. This point cannot be overemphasized.

Communicators' use of body, voice, and eyes consistent with their emotional memory for message effectiveness becomes our next consideration.

Body

Most Christian communicators deliver their message before a "live" audience. As few as twenty or as many as ten thousand may be in attendance. Although much of what has been said so far could be used for those on radio and television, the focus of this book is on "live" communication. In these situations, seekers not only hear but observe the speaker. Unlike radio or television, there are no commercials or retakes. And, most importantly, the one who speaks is usually well known to the audience.

Communicating with one's body is basic to everyday human living. For instance, observe human interaction in a mall, crowded park, or busy airport. Watch how people talk, gesture, and use their hands. Emotion is communicated through body, face, and eyes. This is so natural that we only stop to reflect on it when discussing communication or standing before a group to speak. Then many worry, become self-conscious, and experience anxiety wondering if normal movement is appropriate. The natural "body/word" integration characteristic of thousands of conversations is split and replaced by "zombie-like" use of the body when one is speaking before an audience. Rather than helping to communicate, the body becomes a "drag" on the words. Contemporary Christian communicators seek to use the body in effective ways to facilitate the message. Three factors determine whether the body is a "drag" or "facilitator" and whether the body is used in a natural or unnatural way.

a. *It is most important to seek congruence between emotional memory, message content, and bodily movement.* The most genuine body movements (gestures) come when some aspect of one's emotional memory is evoked by the text and conveyed to the audience. The feelings are natural and, as in normal conversation, the body expresses them in a natural way. For instance, in most informal conversations, body, eyes, and voice are congruent with the emotion of the words. If congruence is absent, most people begin to question the integrity of the words and the sincerity of the speaker. Seekers make the same value judgment about Christian communicators. Few communicators are so emotionally out of touch, devoid of authentic feelings, or boring that they can't link the text with themselves.

b. *Bodily movement is often a function of general health.* Illness, pain, fatigue, depression, injury, and poor posture affects voice production and body movements.

Several years ago I had knee surgery and, after a couple of days in the hospital, returned to my pastoral work. Two or three days after surgery, like a good martyr, I was in the pulpit. Bandages from my hip to ankle immobilized my leg and I had to be helped onto the platform. The next Sunday I used crutches and the following week progressed to a cane. I remember that I could not move normally, so all movements and gestures were less animated and more painful. I had to speak differently. Movement and passion were limited.

On another occasion I conducted a wedding when I had a high fever. Perspiration dripped from my face, smudging my notes. I felt so ill that I barely functioned. Communicating when one is sick, hurt, or physically challenged becomes a struggle, and speakers need to know that physical health does determine how one is able to use one's body.

c. *Regardless of physical health or limitations, effective body movement comes from a triangle: emotional memory, personality, and the text.* Emotional memory must be called forth by the text and the message delivered in ways consistent with one's personality.

One of the big mistakes often made is to design gestures or bodily movement. What needs to happen first is for speakers to be observant of their own feelings and impulses generated by the text/subject.[6] They can then organize and deliver the message around their own feelings and observations. The result will be the use of body, eyes, and voice in a natural "your way" style.

Unlike some, I don't teach how one should gesture or move one's body. Rather, I coach students on how to use their body more effectively. As a professor of communication, I can teach students message content and organization. But I can only coach them in connection and speaking with heart, soul, and passion. As my students speak, I often point out inappropriate, inconsistent, or ineffective use of their body. I encourage them to relax. What I can't do is train people in gestures and body movement because these are a product of the interaction of text and emotional memory.

One technique I often use is to compare a student in normal conversation with the student delivering a message in class. Sometimes I will stop students in class or conversation and tell them to look at themselves. It's who they are in real life that needs to be displayed before the audience when they speak. Not everything in bodily movement is situational. There are four guidelines that all should use in ways congruent with their personality and emotional memory.

1. Increase Intensity

Public speaking requires greater intensity in voice, eye contact, and body movement than normal, *regular* conversation. On one hand we want to be natural. On the other, before an audience, we must project increased intensity in order to communicate.

2. Relax!

Relax! Take deep breaths before speaking. Stretch your back, legs, and arms before going to the platform. If possible, yawn! It's a good way to take a breath. Stretching, yawning, and deep breathing relax the entire body.

3. Be Yourself

Don't be afraid to be yourself. Always remember Brooks's definition of effective preaching: Preaching is communicating truth through personality. The more your personality shines through your speaking, the better, up to the point where your quirks and dysfunctions adversely affect the message.

4. Adapt Body Movement

Adapt body movement to the situation. There is generally less body movement in formal occasions such as funerals, weddings, or academic convocations than evangelistic services or talks at retreats. Tables 14 and 15 outline effective and ineffective use of the body.

Table 14

Effective Use of Body Movement

1. Be relaxed.
2. Be definite.
3. Be appropriate.
4. Be yourself.
5. Use variety.
6. Adapt movement to audience.

Source: Steve and Susan Beebe, *Public Speaking: An Audience-Centered Approach*

Table 15

Ineffective Use of Body Movement

1. Random movement
2. Nervous pacing
3. Shifting weight
4. Adjusting clothes
5. Fiddling with keys, money, or wallet

Source: Jeff Cook, *The Elements of Speech Writing and Public Speaking*

Voice

The voice is to Christian communication what the engine is to the automobile. Nothing happens unless both work. Voice is the most important part of message delivery.[7] It is the physiological engine that makes oral communication possible. Throughout this book I have called attention to the points at which seekers make judgments about the speaker. Sometimes it involves the beginning of a message. Other times it involves the content, connection, or organization of a message or whether there is congruence between emotions, content, and bodily movement. Seekers make judgments on voice quality as well. Often the speaker's intelligence, health, and social and educational backgrounds are judged on the quality of the voice.[8] This may not be fair but it is reality. The good news is that much can be done to improve voice quality. The issue, then, is to learn how to use the voice for maximum effectiveness.

This section cannot deal with all problems relating to voice usage. About 10 percent of the American population suffers serious speech abnormalities. Included are those with cleft palates, voice disorders, and severe articulatory defects such as stuttering and lisping. To make significant improvement, they will need professional help. There are many who, although their voice is physiologically sound, nevertheless use their voice improperly. This book will not help them either, but a speech coach or speech pathologist may. I do hope to raise, however, awareness on important voice concerns that may be helpful, beginning with how sound is produced.

The Physiology of Sound

Contrary to popular opinion, sound is not hearing. Rather, hearing is a result of sound. Sound is a physical event in which acoustic energy is generated. Hearing is the way the body (outer ear, middle ear, inner ear, nervous system, and brain) receives this acoustic energy and changes it into meaningful nerve impulses in the brain. Three components create sound: force, vibration, and medium.[9]

a. *Force.* Breath is the force that creates sound. Air is taken into the lungs and forced out again. When a person decides to speak, the brain sends a message to the vocal folds. Air in the lungs builds pressure below the vocal folds.

b. *Vibration.* Air pressure below the vocal folds increases until it overcomes the muscular forces holding the folds closed. As the air escapes in very rapid bursts, it creates waves of sound above the vocal folds. After each burst, the air pressure decreases and the vocal folds close. Although these waves of sound constitute the human voice, it is still just a vibratory "buzz" of inadequate and inaudible tones. It is still in the larynx (the structure that produces voice at the uppermost part of the trachea).

c. *Medium.* As the sound passes through the throat, teeth, hard palate (roof of the mouth), soft palate (the soft, movable, rear parts of the roof of the mouth), the nose, sinus cavities (located near the nose and eyes), and the forehead, the sound becomes more resonant. In other words, the vibratory buzz is now amplified, strengthened, and beautified. The facial movements of the lips, tongue, and soft palate clearly form sounds that create words, phrases, and larger units of thought. From the mouth words are directed to the audience. This cycle begins and continues as long as an individual wants to speak.[10]

Most Christian communicators want to improve their voice dynamics. How can this be done? Since the production of sound is such a complex physiological and psychological process, improved vocal dynamics depends on individual needs and problems. The following points identify common areas in which voice quality may be improved.

a. *Pitch.* Pitch is the highness or lowness of sound. It is the comfortable zone or range of the voice among octaves. The range of great singers is three and sometimes four octaves. The range of most speakers is only one octave. Three mistakes are often made with pitch. Some speak too high, some too low, and others don't vary their pitch at all. Little pitch variation is called monotone. A monotone voice is distracting to listeners and is associated with boredom.

Paul Eckman shows that when people are angry, fearful, or excited, their pitch rises.[11] When they are sad, their pitch lowers.[12] In ordinary conversation, most people speak in midrange between bass and treble.

Christian communicators should use all the notes of the octave without going lower or higher than their range. Slower speech usually brings the pitch down. More rapid speech raises pitch. Pitch should be a function of emotion and content. Two principles should be observed: stay within your range and constantly vary the pitch based on emotion and content.

b. *Diction*. Diction is the effective or ineffective production of sounds and words when one is speaking. It has to do with clarity and articulation. Most poor diction is due to laziness, nervousness, or too rapid speech. The result is slurring words, mumbling, allowing words to fade, failing to sufficiently pronounce t's and d's, and failing to pronounce the last letters or syllables of words. Poor diction is more than just a failure of speech. Seekers perceive those who speak too softly as less decisive, less intelligent, and less informed. Those who mumble are perceived as ethically questionable.[13] Mumbling creates the impression of evasion—hiding information and lacking candor. Diction problems are corrected by concentrating, slowing the speaking rate, using the whole range of vocal production (voice, diaphragm, and chest), and continuing to work on congruence between words and emotion. A speech pathologist should be consulted if efforts at self-improvement fall short.

c. *Rate*. The rate of speech is the number of words spoken per minute.[14] How fast should one speak? What is the proper rate? Rate in normal conversation is between 200 and 300 words per minute. That is too fast for messages. Most presidential candidates speak between 150 and 170 words per minute.[15] The rate of Martin Luther King Jr.'s "I Have a Dream" speech was 92 words per minute at the beginning and 145 at the end. John F. Kennedy was quick paced. He often spoke at a rate of 180 words per minute.[16] Radio commercials are read at a rate of 125 words per minute. If the most heavily coached speakers of our day (presidential candidates) have set a rate pattern of 150 to 170 words per minute, Christian communicators would be wise to follow their example. But rate for Christian communicators should be a function of message content and speaking style. Listeners understand faster than a speaker can produce words. However, four conclusions can be drawn. First, the rate should be increased when things are important or exciting. Second, the rate should be decreased when one is emphasizing key points or ideas. Third, the rate should match the emotional content of the message. Fourth, when the rate does not match the emotion of the words, the message will be discounted.[17]

If Christian communicators want to work on voice quality, we must understand that our ear is not a good guide. One hears one's own voice through bone conduction, not air conduction. When someone speaks, sound goes through the air to the hearer's ear. When one hears oneself, vibration goes through the bone of the cranium. Since voice is heard through air conduction, our own ear is not an adequate or accurate judge to evaluate our own voice. This is one reason why bad speech habits are so hard to break. We are either too harsh or too easy on the quality of our voice.[18] An audiotape or videotape of one's message is a more accurate indicator of voice quality than one's own evaluation.

In the end, nervousness is most often the culprit behind poor voice quality. Table 16 summarizes how to deal with nervousness before and during a message.

Table 16

Dealing with Nervousness

1. Slow the rate.
2. Rotate your shoulders.
3. Take deep breaths from your abdomen.
4. Stretch your upper body.

Source: Roger Axtell, *Do's and Taboos of Public Speaking*

---

d. *Pause.* A pause is a short stop in the message. It is an effective way to communicate a point and to relax for a brief second. It can signal that what was said is important. It allows listeners to ponder an idea or feeling. If a pause follows a question, listeners will answer it for themselves. A pause is often most effectively used after making an important point and before or after transitions.

Table 17 summarizes some of the cardinal concerns of voice usage in Christian communication, and Table 18 matches voice problems with possible solutions.

Table 17
Important Questions in Message Delivery

1. Is it loud enough?
2. Is the rate appropriate?
3. Is it clear?
4. Is the pitch pleasant?
5. Are there frequent pauses?
6. Is there pitch variety?

Source: Jeff Cook, *The Elements of Speech Writing and Public Speaking*

Table 18
Voice Problems and Solutions

Problem	Solution
1. Too high pitch	Slow rate.
2. Too low pitch	Increase rate.
3. Monotone voice	Vary pitch.
4. Voice too harsh, tense	Relax voice by breathing; pause.
5. Need more excitement	Increase rate and pitch.
6. Need to emphasize important points	Lower rate and pitch; pause.
7. Nervousness	Pause; breathe deeply; stretch muscles.
8. Mumbling	Slow rate.

Eyes

Jesus emphasized the importance of the eyes: "'The eye is the lamp of the whole body. So, if your eye is healthy, your whole body will be full of light; but if your eye is unhealthy, your whole body will be full of darkness'" (Matthew 6:22, 23). In this passage the eye is a metaphor for living an ethical or unethical life. Jesus' understanding of the eye reflects a widespread cross-cultural phenomenon. Eyes are the windows to the soul or the reflection of one's innermost being.[19] The eyes as well as the face have a large capacity for nonverbal communication. Steven and Susan Beebe say human beings are capable of producing over a quarter of a million different facial expressions. Facial response to the primary emotions of happiness, sadness, anger, surprise, disgust, fear, and interest are accurately "read" by others even across cultural and situational lines.[20] This suggests that a universal language of facial expression transcends language and culture. If the face and primarily the eyes have this kind of power, contemporary communicators must understand how to utilize them.

The eyes are the most important component of facial expression. Research on eye contact indicates that eyes invite or indicate intimacy.[21] Eye contact initiates a dialogical relationship. It bonds people and creates a sense of community.[22] When listeners look at the speaker, they indicate that they want to be included. When the speaker looks back, listeners sense that they are being included in the message.[23] The effective use of eyes builds community and intimacy with listeners.

As a general maxim of interpersonal relationships, those who avoid eye contact are perceived as uncaring, dishonest, and emotionally distant. Those with good eye contact are judged to be sincere, attentive, and respectful.[24] But good eye contact not only builds interpersonal bridges to seekers, it also helps determine whether message content "makes sense." By looking at seekers and making eye contact for a few seconds, an invitation is given. The speaker can discern a listener's reaction to the message when their eyes meet. Through their eye and facial expressions seekers will often tell the speaker if the message is confusing or boring. Often eyes tell whether someone agrees or disagrees with the message.

We can readily see why eye contact is important. Eye contact opens communication with listeners, provides listener reaction, gives moral credibility to the speaker, and keeps listeners' interest.[25]

Effective Eye Contact

Before effective eye contact can be practiced, bad habits must be corrected. Eye contact is *not* staring at individuals. For most people in Western culture, being stared at is uncomfortable. It is interpreted as a threat to one's safety.[26] Eye contact is *not* bobbing and weaving one's eyes around the room like a politician "making the rounds." Further, it is *not* an exercise of a puppy dog begging and pleading for the audience to listen.

The best way to achieve effective eye contact is to think of the audience as individuals. Therefore, *never* gaze over people's heads, but always be specific. As you speak, look directly at a pair of eyes for a few seconds, then move to another, then to another. Don't allow your eyes to jump helter-skelter. Look. Make a statement. Move your eyes. Make another statement. Don't look at people; *visit* them! As you visit them with your eyes, they will respond to you and your message with their eyes.

How long should you look at each person? Research indicates that you can speak one complete thought and sustain eye contact for at least five seconds and maintain a favorable impact on the audience.[27]

Authenticity, Passion and Seekers

Barb's struggle with the messages from her church does not concern content or connection but the speaker's authenticity. The infomercial, steps-to-happiness messages discourage seekers from understanding or dealing with the dislocations of their lives. But Barb refuses to deny the pain she is living. Rather than providing perspective, perseverance, and hope for her pain, the messages alienate her from her pain and from others in the church. How can there be fellowship and support when everyone has to be happy all the time?

Barb is like millions of seekers. They simply will not tolerate or listen to a speaker who seems divorced from life's dislocations and pain. Speakers must be authentic! Authentic communicators are honest ones; they're the same whether they're speaking publicly or privately. They honestly embrace their pain, doubts, and shortcomings. Authenticity is not so much something that comes by what we do but rather by what we become. In oral communication it comes from the courage to use one's emotional memory in the message.

Barb likes her pastor. He is a genuinely nice and caring person. He works hard. However, his messages miss her life, pain, and questions. Why? Maybe he is afraid to be human. Maybe he is afraid to face his pain. Maybe he thinks those who communicate the Christian faith should be above life's struggles. But Barb's life is like Humpty Dumpty's. It has been shattered. She doesn't expect the king's horses and men, but she would like help from Sunday's messages in putting the pieces together again. But then again, after five years of this pastor's messages, she wonders if anything in his life has ever been shattered; not even a hair is out of place!

Chapter 9

Message Planning: What? Why? How?

Pastor Lynn Smith slowly trudges into the study. It is 9:00 Monday morning. Yesterday was a typical Sunday filled with meetings, teaching, and speaking, which have left Smith tired. After pouring a cup of coffee, Lynn reviews yesterday's statistics. The offering was good, which brings a smile and a warm feeling. But attendance at both Sunday school and worship was down. Lynn ponders why. Putting the "stat sheet" aside, a second cup of coffee joins the appointment book on the table. Tonight is a church board meeting, a small-group leaders' training event is planned for early tomorrow morning, and Bible study fills Wednesday night. Counseling appointments are spread throughout the week; and several members are hospitalized. Although small-group leaders provide most of the pastoral care for members, Lynn still likes to visit and pray with those in the hospital.

The full schedule makes Lynn anxious. What am I going to say this Sunday? Where am I going to find time for study and message preparation? Every year Lynn resolves to plan ahead, manage time better, and dedicate at least a day a week for study and message preparation. Like most diets, this works for a while, but good habits are hard to establish.

If you scratch below Lynn's jovial and caring surface, you will find a minister who is living with high levels of stress and is on the brink of burnout. The constant push and relentless grind of producing a message every seven days is one of the chief reasons for the stress. Late Saturday afternoon, weary after a long workweek; angry at omnipresent, time-consuming human needs; and feeling guilty that better messages are not offered to God and the people of the church, Lynn once again throws together a message.

The experience of Pastor Lynn is not unlike many pastors, teaching pastors, and youth leaders. Most ministers struggle with what to talk about each Sunday and few have a disciplined approach to message preparation and study. Deciding what topic to discuss is more difficult for those who speak to the same people every seven days. Traveling speakers, evangelists, or occasional speakers do not have this problem. They simply work up a dozen messages and shape them to the audience.

The one who speaks forty to fifty times per year (double or triple this number if the church expects messages on Wednesday and/or Sunday evenings) has a difficult task. Even pastors of the largest churches don't have speech writers and most are involved in many church leadership activities, plus pastoral care and counseling.

In light of the unique communication demands most pastors face, this chapter attempts to answer three questions:

1. What should my message be about?
2. What is the benefit of planning ahead?
3. How do I go about message planning?

What Should My Message Be About?

Like the proverbial broken record, I again affirm that the Bible is the anchor and content for communicating with seekers. Using crisscross interpretation the speaker crosses from the Bible to a seeker concern, demonstrating Scripture's wisdom or perspective on the concern or vice versa. In one sense the question, What should my message be about? is already answered. We find what we say in the Bible. However, an additional step helps to focus biblical teaching on seeker needs. The following questions may provide the step toward determining what to say:

1. What are the important issues seekers face in their everyday lives?

2. What are the most pressing needs in the church and community?
3. What are the most pressing international and national needs at the moment?
4. What are the most significant moral, ethical, and spiritual questions of the day?
5. What burdens and bothers the mind and heart of the communicator?
6. What biblical teaching needs to be presented?
7. How can I ensure that a complete biblical message is communicated?

There are several ways the communicator may answer these questions in order to plan messages. First, sit down, pen in hand, and list the needs, concerns, and problems of seekers in general and those in the church specifically. On everyone's list will be racism, the environment, addictions, loneliness, sex, insecurity, fear, sin, guilt, hate, stress, burnout, love, doubt, failure, despair, conflict, sickness, child rearing, marriage, divorce, friendship, relationships, stepfamilies, singleness, grief, evil, suffering, poverty, death, ethics, and many social problems. Then look for how the Bible addresses these questions.

Perhaps the best way to discover seeker needs, problems, and concerns is to ask seekers. Survey Sunday morning attenders ask them what is on their hearts and minds. Tell them to send their responses by phone, fax, mail, or E-mail to the church. Generally this exercise will yield more great ideas for messages than can be used.

The calendar is also useful for planning messages. Often holidays and special days provide ways to demonstrate what the Bible says about important cultural events. Table 19 lists some special days with appropriate message subjects.

Table 19
Special-Day Messages for Seekers

Day	Subject
Labor Day	Being a Christian in the Marketplace
Mid-September (start of school)	The Importance of Education
Halloween	The Occult, Demons, or Satan
Election Day	Church and State
Thanksgiving	Giving Thanks When Your Heart Is Breaking
New Year's	New Beginnings
Valentine's Day	Dating; Marriage; Sex; Relationships; Being Single in a Couples' World
Mother's Day	Being a Working or Single Mother
Graduation	Passages and Transitions
Father's Day	Being a Father—How?
Summer	Recreation

These subject suggestions are merely illustrative of the general direction a message may take. Many communicators have retreated from developing messages about holidays and special days. They do so for good reason. In the past, special-day messages were often trite. In some cases Mother's Day, Father's Day, and Election Day messages embarrassed the audience. However, special-day messages can be reclaimed and given a fresh twist. They present an excellent opportunity to say something relevant about relationships, education, work, recreation, transitions, and new beginnings. Seekers will recall the occasion and the message subject together.

A third way to communicate the whole biblical message is to speak on Christian doctrine. Since speaking on doctrine was so poorly done in the past, "doctrine" and "boring" have become synonyms. But subjects like God, Jesus, the future, the Holy Spirit, the church, and the importance of the Bible are appealing to seekers.

We may underestimate the intelligence of the average seeker. No seeker goes to a car dealership expecting a concert or to a bookstore expecting to work out. With great demands on their time, seekers would not bother to come to a church if they wanted a circus. Rather, they expect the church to do what it is supposed to do—namely, point to and honestly deal with the spiritual aspects of life. If seekers do go to church and the spiritual dimension is missing or hidden, they will feel ripped off and misled. In their mind they will perceive that another American institution has violated its stated purpose.

Speaking on Christian doctrine is not offensive to seekers; they expect it. But if doctrine is the subject of a message, the speaker has the burden to show how it is relevant to seekers and to explain it creatively and intelligently.

Another reason for speaking on doctrine comes from an interesting source. Psychologist Carl Jung noted that *all* of his patients in the second half of life became ill because they lost their spiritual moorings and *none* were healed until they regained their religious outlook. Jung was asked to explain. In a 1959 letter he said that every culture throughout history has had a general teaching or doctrine about the wholeness of the world. In the West this has been the Christian plausibility structure and doctrine (see chapter 3). However, over the last one hundred years Christian doctrine "has lost its grip to an appalling extent, chiefly because people don't understand it anymore."[1]

What Jung seems to be saying is that the irrelevance of Christian doctrine has created a culture of seekers who, after losing their spiritual anchor or never having had one, are seeking psychological help in their search for meaning. The relevant proclamation of Christian doctrine might be the key to helping seekers find meaning and wholeness in their lives. Jung seems to indicate that Christian doctrine is more than information. It literally transforms lives.

Another way to determine what your message should be about is to consult the lectionary. The lectionary is a three-year cycle of Bible readings that covers the main events of the life of Israel and Jesus, the major Christian doctrines, and the major seasons of the church year (Advent, Christmas, Epiphany, Lent, Holy Week, Easter, Pentecost). Each of the three years centers on a different Gospel. Readings from the Gospel of John are interspersed throughout the year. There are four readings (lections) for each Sunday of the year—a psalm, an Old Testament reading, a Gospel reading, and one from an Epistle. Those using the lectionary say it broadens the range of texts for messages, forces them to wrestle with texts they would otherwise avoid, and underscores the primacy of biblical teaching, thus reducing an excessive concern for relevance or pet peeves.[2]

Finally, picking a book of the Bible and in effect creating your own lectionary is a way to determine what your message should be about. The most important question for planning an expository, systematic series from a book of the Bible concerns the purpose, reason, or occasion this book was written. For instance, the letter to the Romans is an orderly presentation of Paul's gospel written to clarify misunderstandings and raise support from the church at Rome to evangelize Spain (Romans 1:13; 15:22, 24, 28). In 1 Corinthians Paul responds in writing to six questions church leaders asked him in a prior letter. These questions were about marriage (7:1), singleness (7:25-26), meat sacrificed to idols (8:1), spiritual gifts (12:1), money (16:1), and Apollos's visit (16:12). He also wrote to deal with the problem of a personality cult and to appeal to unity in the midst of church conflict (1:12-13; 3:1-8, 18-23; 4:6). Luke stresses that his Gospel is for the poor, lost, and forgotten. In other words, Luke wrote to seekers—especially those who have been bruised and marginalized by organized religion (i.e., the church).

The point of illustrating with Romans, 1 Corinthians, and Luke is to reiterate that any single passage of any book of the Bible must be understood based on the purpose of the book. The reason, purpose, or occasion of the book always determines how a passage is interpreted and thus connected. One must understand the whole to understand the parts. The following table summarizes sources for message topics.

Table 20

Speaking to Seekers: Sources for Message Topics

1. Series on seeker's needs
2. Special days of the year
3. Christian doctrine
4. Lectionary readings
5. Section-by-section passages from Bible books

To Plan or Not to Plan . . .

Henry Ward Beecher was one of America's best preachers and foremost clergy members of the nineteenth century. He had a simple method of message planning. He chose the text and subject of his message on Sunday morning. Any preparation that was done occurred between the time the text and subject were selected and when the church bell rang.[3] At the other extreme was Harry Emerson Fosdick. Like Beecher, he was a great preacher of the first half of this century. He supposedly spent one hour of study for every minute in the pulpit. These two examples say something unsettling: excellent communicators have different methods of message preparation. If Fosdick's discipline seems too rigorous, why not follow Beecher? Why bother to think seriously about message planning?

There are several reasons every speaker should develop a careful method of message planning. First, the challenge of speaking to seekers demands subject competence. There may have been a time when one could "slide by," giving only a meager effort. That day is long gone. Talk shows, radio, television, computers, and advances in education have produced a generation that is much more aware and knowledgeable than its predecessors. Therefore, when someone speaks to seekers, that person must have the facts straight. The only way to gain competence is to commit oneself to a life of study. Study and preparation are core commitments for those who speak to seekers. Gardner C. Taylor is correct: sustained excellent preaching comes only through effort and anguish caused by study and preparation.[4]

The search for knowledge, insight, and understanding is an ongoing process. One does not rely on seminary or graduate education to provide subject competence. Rather, college, graduate, and seminary education should give the speaker skills and discipline to think, read, and reflect about message subjects. Taylor's thinking should be taken one step further: there is no room for seeker communicators who do not want to think and study hard. If you are unwilling to study and think, find another avenue of ministry. Seekers will see through a thin veneer of piety and weak attempts to deal with life-shaking issues. Why should any seeker listen to someone who disrespects them by not wrestling with their questions and pain in an intellectually honest way?

There is also a practical payoff for diligent study. From a cost/benefit analysis, effective messages provide the biggest "bang for the buck," regardless of the size of the church. The Sunday morning service is usually the best-attended event of the church week. What is said and done there affects the whole ministry. If only a hundred people attend and the message is thirty minutes long, the total time investment is fifty hours. That exceeds an average workweek and is too many hours to waste; seeker schedules are too full. The Sunday morning message (Saturday evening in some churches), then, must be both good and effective.

I believe there is a direct link between study and message effectiveness. Lack of study is perhaps the most significant reason for anemic content and lackluster connection. Sufficient study improves both, and the whole congregation benefits. Always remember, study does not take one *away* from people; rather, it is a way to better understand and connect *with* people.

The first reason to plan messages is to ensure the adequate study time necessary for effective speaking to seekers. Second, the nature of church ministry demands effective message planning. Working on a church staff can permit great schedule flexibility as compared to working in other jobs and professions. Working hours, days off, and schedule details may be at one's own discretion. On the other hand, most ministers are like Lynn Smith. Similar to firefighters' schedules, ministers' schedules are often dictated by the demands of others. Although flexible, the schedule is easily tyrannized. If the speaker does not discipline his or her schedule by establishing blocks of time for message preparation, no one else will. There is always another imperative task, a call to make, or a need to be met. These cry for immediate attention. Study time only whispers and is easily and often ignored. No wonder there are so many Saturday-night specials!

Third, message planning aids worship and program planning. The message is one part of a larger package. Music, drama, singing, liturgy, and interviews or testimonies are all part of the service, although this book has discussed only the message. Planning ahead helps the worship team be more creative and effective in coordinating these other important parts of the service.

Finally, planning enhances creativity and imagination in messages. For our purpose it is important to note that the brain operates in two ways, what some have called left- and right-brain functioning. Certain current researchers contend that the left side of the brain gathers facts and information and engages in verbal, analytical, rational, symbolic, and abstract functioning. The left hemisphere is concerned with logic.

The right hemisphere of the brain is the sensing, intuitive side. It creates new perceptions and insights and is the place of imagination and creativity. In some ways the right side takes information and facts from the left and manipulates them, creating new relationships, new combinations of "colors" and new "colors" from existing ones.[5] Craig Skinner maintains that the right brain makes connections and brings fresh relevance to the left brain's factual information.[6]

As mysterious as this sounds, most humans have experienced right- and left-brain functioning. For instance, suppose you hear about a job opening that you would like to explore. You begin to write a letter of inquiry. Your first draft goes badly. You can't quite say what you want. The ideas don't flow and the sentence structure is choppy. After the third draft you put the letter down and decide to read the Sunday comics. In the midst of "Peanuts," seemingly from nowhere comes a brilliant insight about what to say and how to say it. You sprint across the living room, tripping over the cat, desperate to write the words before they disappear. As you scribble the last clause you think, This is a great letter!

While you were composing the letter, your left brain was at work. When in frustration you put it away, your right brain subconsciously began to do its creative and imaginative work with the data. The flash of insight came from the right brain. The result was a letter with different "colors and hues."

Message planning and preparation must use both left- and right-brain functions. Content is a left-brain activity while connection and emotional memory come from the right brain. Reading, studying, and reflection engage the left brain. But accumulating the data and information is not enough. Messages that present information without creativity fail to connect with seekers. Often they are written too late in the week for the right brain to do its work. Or, the speaker has not allowed the material to "simmer" in his or her right brain.

Like the employment letter, most messages get stuck during preparation. Authors call this "writer's block." As a general rule, when the message is not coming, a person should change activities. Read the comics or a book, listen to music, go running, work in the yard, or play a game with the children. This change would be difficult at 7:30 p.m. on Saturday and argues for scheduled study and preparation that anticipates occasional blocks. Doing something else gives the right brain time to creatively synthesize the information. This leads to insight and imaginative flashes of relevant material.

Return with me for a moment to the Italian-American neighborhood in which I grew up. There, many have retained the proud cooking traditions of Italy and Sicily. At the heart of this cuisine is tomato sauce, and making this sauce is almost a religious ceremony. Only the best ingredients are purchased and the tomatoes are preferably homegrown. Every part of the family recipe, handed down from the Old Country, is carefully followed because the process is almost as important as the ingredients. When all the ingredients are combined in the correct order, the sauce simmers all day so that the flavor of the sausage blends with the oregano, garlic, and tomatoes. The right combination of ingredients, simmered slowly, produces an exquisite sauce. (I can taste it as I write!)

The application for message preparation and brain functioning is direct. Study both creates the ingredients and puts them into the left brain. Time and attention to feelings and impressions turn the ingredients into a well-blended, appealing message!

Several ingredients are now ready to assemble into the message. Connection and emotional memory come from the right brain. Since connection, authenticity, and emotional memory are so important to seekers, a method of message preparation that balances left-brain fact-finding with right-brain functioning must be developed. An effective message can't be served when ingredients are missing.

How to Plan and Prepare Messages

Message planning for seekers takes place in two stages. In the first stage the communicator must get away four times during the year for a day or two (retreat center, college library, public library, community room, hospital conference room, etc.) to plan messages for the quarter ahead. This "getaway" should take place in July for the fall quarter, October for the winter quarter, January for the spring quarter, and April for the summer quarter.

In each general planning session key questions should be answered:

1. What went well last quarter?
2. What went poorly?
3. What must be done to improve the quality of the messages?
4. What subjects need to be addressed this quarter?
5. Is the church reaching its goals?
6. What should the message priorities be for this upcoming quarter?
7. What special days this quarter deserve a message?

After answering these questions, the communicator is ready to consult the list of seeker needs and determine what Bible books or doctrines should be included in this quarter's messages. The next step is to create a message planning sheet (table 21) that includes the date, text, subject, and ideas. The idea section is an important space on the message planning sheet. Here any thoughts, feelings, message statements, goals, sources, illustrations, or possible move patterns are noted. When you plan a quarter of messages your right brain will constantly generate insights and ideas about various messages. Record them in the idea section. If you read articles or studies or find illustrations, they should be placed in file folders for future reference.

How does the message planning sheet work in practice? During the fall quarter of 1994 I did two message series. The first was "Institutions that Shape Our Lives," followed by a three-part series on 1 John. Table 21 shows the planning sheet I prepared.

Table 21

Fall 1994 Message Planning Sheet

Date	Text	Subject	Ideas
September 11	II Thessalonians 3:6-15	Work	
September 18	Proverbs 4:1-9	Education	
September 25	Deuteronomy 6:1-9	Family	
October 2	Revelation 22:1-9	Church	

Series One on 1 John: "What is the Christian Faith?"

October 9	1 John 3:11-20	Love	
October 16	1 John 1:5-7	Obedience	
October 23	1 John 4:1-6	Jesus	

Series Two on 1 John: "Life Busters"

October 30	1 John 2:15-25	The Occult	
November 6	1 John 2:7-14	Hate: Racism	
November 13	1 John 2:15-17	Church and Culture	

Series Three on 1 John: "But What If We Fail?"

November 20	1 John 1:8-10; 2:1-2	Honesty and Confession	
November 27	1 John 3:21-24	Boundaries: Love, Faith, Obedience	
December 1	1 John 5:13-15	Prayer	

By following a quarterly plan you will help yourself know what to say and when to say it. This quarterly general plan encourages both left- and right-brain functioning. Left-brain analysis is done far enough ahead to allow the right brain to bring connection and emotional memory. There is also enough time for thorough study. You now can focus your study on the subject, Bible books, and texts of the message.

The second stage of message planning is a weekly message preparation schedule. Three factors must be considered before scheduling weekly message preparation time. First, time blocks for message preparation must be created. Second, Wardlaw says that preachers who care deeply about preaching spend about twelve to fourteen hours per week on their message.[7] Third, most methods of message preparation come from college or seminary professors or megachurch pastors. Many of these ideas and methods are helpful, but there are some problems. Seminary professors live in an entirely different environment than do individuals in church ministry. Their observations about how to prepare will reflect this difference. The methods of megachurch pastors work for them but may not work for you. Their method is based on their gifts but may not be practical for someone with other gifts.

Michael Jordan could help me improve my jump shot, but no amount of practice would permit me to beat him in a game of "horse." Why? Because I don't have Jordan's athletic abilities. I could learn from him but I doubt I will ever "be like Mike." Some megachurch pastors are like Mike. One can learn from them but what they do and how they do it engages their gifts. You may not have the same gifts and will be disappointed with the results. What is needed, then, is a weekly schedule that is flexible enough for different temperaments but specific enough so that there are at least twelve hours of study per week. To enhance right-brain creativity the twelve hours should be spread over several days. Following is a suggested weekly message preparation schedule of five time blocks over a seven-day period. Each block states a goal to be accomplished during that time period. Two days have no set message preparation activity. This is an attempt to encourage creativity in messages by allowing time for right-brain functioning.

Block 1: Monday, 9:00 a.m. to 12:00 noon, three hours

The goal for the first hour and one-half is to work on *next* week's message. Identify the subject and make a preliminary message statement and goal. Determine what sources, information, and material you will need to complete the message *next* week.

The goal for the last hour and one-half is to work on this Sunday's message. Read commentaries, study important words, read the text out loud, and visualize what might have happened. Review the subject, message statement, and goal from your preliminary work the week before. Does it need revision?

Block 2: Tuesday, 9:00 a.m. to 12:00 noon, three hours

The goal of this session is to determine the subject, message statement, goal, and move pattern (chapter 6). Continue studying until you can write the subject, message statement, and goal with unwavering clarity. Work on connection. What are your feelings about the subject? What is coming from your emotional memory? Over the next two days don't work on the message, but note your feelings and insights.

Block 3: Thursday, 9:00 a.m. to 12:00 noon, three hours

The goal of this session is to put the entire message together. Settle on the subject, message statement, goal, and move pattern. Are there illustrations or insights that should be included in the message? What needs to be deleted? Once this is complete, write the beginning and ending. If there is time, start your study for next week's message.

Block 4: Friday, 9:00 a.m. to 12:00 noon, three hours

The goal of this session is to have the message "pulpit ready." In other words, by the end of this period, whatever you use in the pulpit—manuscript or notes—should be ready to go.

Block 5: Sunday morning, one hour

The goal of this session is to review or practice the message aloud. Don't be surprised if several good ideas emerge. This comes from the right brain and emotional memory.

The reader should feel free to shape, rearrange, or change this weekly message preparation schedule. Personalize it! However, shortening the blocks or skipping the time for creativity will damage both message content and connection.

Epilogue

But will it all work? If a message has biblical content that connects to seekers, and if the communicator speaks with passion, soul, and creativity, will Raymond, Barb, and Susan find meaningful community, leave the seeker ranks, and find their place in today's church? It takes more than messages to bring Raymond back into community, to deal with Barb's pain, and to answer Susan's ethical dilemma.

Church ministry is much more than just speaking. However, relevant, biblical messages that connect do change people and communities. Who knows? Someday you may be the one with a relevant life-changing word to Raymond, Barb, and Susan! As they change, the church and society will also change. Oh, what a day that will be!

Notes

Introduction

1. Kenneth L. Woodward, "Dead End for the Mainline," *Newsweek*, August 9, 1993; 23: 46-48.

2. For a good discussion on revival, renewal, and its impact on church and society, see William G. McLoughlin, *Revivals, Awakenings, and Reform* (Chicago: University of Chicago Press, 1978).

Chapter 1

1. David Halberstam, *The Fifties* (New York: Villard Books, 1993), 196-201.

2. Alvin Toffler, *The Third Wave* (New York: William Morrow, 1980), 29.

3. William A. Faunce, *Problems of Industrial Society* (New York: McGraw-Hill, 1968), 15.

4. Ibid., 16.

5. Jacques Ellul, *The Technological Society* (New York: Knopf, 1964), 44.

6. Clark Kerr, et al., *Industrialism and Industrial Man* (New York: Oxford University Press, 1964), 221.

7. Faunce, *Problems of Industrial Society*, 15.

8. Ellul, *The Technological Society*, 44.

9. Lesslie Newbigin, *Foolishness to the Greeks: The Gospel and Western Culture* (Grand Rapids: William B. Eerdmans, 1986), 34.

10. Faunce, *Problems of Industrial Society*, 21.

11. Kerr, et al., *Industrialism and Industrial Man*, 19.

12. Ibid., 23.

13. John Naisbitt, *Megatrends* (New York: Warner Books, 1982), 12-13.

14. Ibid., 12-15.

15. Toffler, *The Third Wave*, 26.

16. Ibid., 38.

17. Thomas G. Fuechtman tells this amazing story in his book *Steeples and Stacks: Religion and the Steel Crises in Youngstown* (Cambridge: Cambridge University Press, 1989).

18. Robert Bellah, et al., *The Good Society* (New York: Knopf, 1991).

Chapter 2

1. Wade Clark Roof, *A Generation of Seekers* (San Francisco: HarperCollins, 1993).

2. Ray Bakke, *International Urban Associates 1994 Ministry Report*.

3. Toffler, *Future Shock* (New York: Random House, 1970), 23.

4. David B. Barrett, "Annual Statistical Table on Global Mission: 1991," *International Bulletin of Missionary Research* 15 (January 1991): 25.

5. Bakke, *International Urban Associates 1994 Ministry Report*.

6. Donna M. Chavez, "Bye, Neighbor: Socializing Slips in the Suburbs," *Chicago Tribune*, 27 March 1994, sec. 18, 3.

7. Paul K. Hatt and Albert J. Reiss, eds., *Cities and Society: A Revised Reader in Urban Sociology* (Glencoe: The Free Press, 1957), 197.

8. Peter Berger, *The Heretical Imperative* (Garden City: Anchor Press, 1979), 98-99.

9. George F. Pozzeta, *American Immigration and Ethnicity: The Immigrant Religious Experience* (New York: Garland, 1991), v.

10. H. Richard Niebuhr, *The Social Sources of Denominationalism* (New York: Henry Holt and Co., 1929).

11. U.S. Immigration and Naturalization Service, *Annual Report*, 1973, and Leonard Dinnerstein and David M. Reimers, *Ethnic Americans: A History of Immigration and Assimilation* (New York: Harper & Row, 1975), 163-170.

12. John H. Franklin, *From Slavery to Freedom: A History of Negro Americans* (New York: Knopf, 1974), 44-45.

13. U.S. Displaced Persons Commission, *The Final Report of the United States Displaced Persons Commission* (Washington, D.C.: GPO, 1952), 1-2.

14. Wade C. Roof and William McKinney, *American Mainline Religion: Its Changing Shape and Future* (New Brunswick: Rutgers University Press, 1987), 117-25.

15. Ibid., 125.

16. David Elkind, *All Grown Up and No Place to Go* (Reading: Addison-Wesley, 1984).

17. Brigitte Berger and Peter Berger, *The War Over the Family* (Garden City: Anchor Press, 1983), 87.

18. Elkind, *All Grown Up and No Place to Go*, 116.

19. James Patterson and Peter Kim, *The Day America Told the Truth* (New York: Prentice Hall, 1991), 3.

20. Ibid., 92.

21. Judy Wallerstein, *Second Chances* (New York: Tickmor & Fields, 1989), ix-xxi.

22. Barbara Schoichet, *The New Single Woman: Discovering a Life of Her Own* (Los Angeles: Howell House, 1994), 24.

23. Wallerstein, 245.

24. Patterson and Kim, *The Day America Told the Truth*, 43, 87.

25. Evelyn Whitehead and James Whitehead, *Marrying Well* (Garden City: Doubleday, 1981), 42.

26. Berger and Berger, *The War Over the Family*, 24.

27. Lee Strobel, *Inside the Mind of Unchurched Harry and Mary* (Grand Rapids: Zondervan, 1993), 76.

Chapter 3

1. Patterson and Kim, *The Day America Told the Truth*, 43.

2. *Religion in America 1992-93* (Princeton Religion Research Center 25th Anniversary Edition), 43.

3. Ibid., 40.

4. Ibid., 42.

5. Patterson and Kim, *The Day America Told the Truth*, 25.

6. *Religion in America 1992-93*, 23.

7. Patterson and Kim, *The Day America Told the Truth*, 200.

8. Berger, *The Heretical Imperative*.

9. Robert Wuthnow, *The Restructuring of American Religion* (Princeton: Princeton University Press, 1988), 20-25.

10. Ibid., 100-131, 173-214.

11. Paul Edwards, ed., *The Encyclopedia of Philosophy* (New York: Macmillan, 1967), 2, 519-25.

12. Berger, *The Heretical Imperative*, 28.

13. Ibid., 49.

14. Ibid., 95-190.

15. Roof and McKinney, *American Mainline Religion*, 233.

16. Ibid., 242.

17. Diogenes Allen, "The End of the Modern World," *Christian Scholar's Review* XXII (June 1993): 339-347. See also Diogenes Allen, "Christianity and the Creed of Post Modernism," *Christian Scholars Review* XXIII (December 1993): 117-126.

18. Ibid., 340.

19. Strobel, *Inside the Mind of Unchurched Harry and Mary*, 80.

20. George Barna, *Never on Sunday: The Challenge of the Unchurched* (Glendale: Barna Research Group, 1990), 1-6.

21. *The Unchurched American*, a Gallup Research Study (1988), 94, 11.

22. Michael Medved and David Wallechinsky, *What Really Happened to the Class of '65?* (New York: Random House, 1976).

23. Dean R. Hoge, Benton Johnson, and Donald Luidens, *Vanishing Boundaries: The Religion of Mainline Protestant Baby Boomers* (Louisville: Westminster/John Knox, 1994).

24. J. Russell Hale, *The Unchurched* (San Francisco: Harper & Row, 1980), 184.

25. Patterson and Kim, *The Day America Told the Truth*, 200, 216.

Chapter 4

1. A. Berkley Mickelsen, *Interpreting the Bible* (Grand Rapids: William B. Eerdmans, 1963), 80-85.

2. Walter M. Abbott, ed., *The Documents of Vatican II* (New York: Crossroad, 1989), 58-118.

3. J. Gordon Melton, *The Encyclopedia of American Religions: Religious Creeds* (Detroit: Cale Research Co., 1989), 148.

4. Ibid., 163.

5. Ibid., 239-40.

6. Ibid., 264.

7. Ibid., 481.

8. W. J. Hollenweger, *The Pentecostals* (Minneapolis: Augsburg Publishing House, 1972), 514.

9. Gilbert Bilezikian, *Christianity 101* (Grand Rapids: Zondervan, 1993).

10. Mickelsen, *Interpreting the Bible*, 5.

11. John H. Hayes and Carl R. Holladay, *Biblical Exegesis: A Beginner's Handbook* (Atlanta: John Knox Press, 1982), 7-18.

12. E. D. Hirsch Jr., *Validity in Interpretation* (New Haven: Yale University Press, 1967), 10.

13. God as Father is a simile. However, all similes are metaphors.

14. Sallie McFague, *Speaking in Parables: A Study in Metaphor and Theology* (Philadelphia: Fortress Press, 1975), 76.

15. Wayne Oates, *When Religion Gets Sick* (Philadelphia: Westminster Press, 1970), 15.

16. McFague, *Speaking in Parables*, 2.

17. Stanley Greidanus, *The Modern Preacher and the Ancient Text: Interpreting and Preaching Biblical Literature* (Grand Rapids: William B. Eerdmans, 1988), 188.

18. Thomas G. Long, *Preaching the Literary Forms of the Bible* (Philadelphia: Fortress Press, 1989), 65-66.

19. Robert Alter, *The Art of Biblical Narrative* (New York: Basic Books, 1981), 33.

20. Long, *Preaching the Literary Forms of the Bible*, 67.

21. Ibid., 74.

22. James E. Massey, *Designing the Sermon: Order and Movement in Preaching* (Nashville: Abingdon Press, 1990), 36. See also Gerhard von Rad, *Old Testament Theology* (New York: Harper & Row, vol. 1, 1962, 105-128.

23. Gerhard von Rad, *Old Testament Theology*, vol. 2 (New York: Harper & Row, 1965), 43.

24. Mickelsen, *Interpreting the Bible*, 286.

25. Greidanus, *The Modern Preacher and the Ancient Text*, 261-67.

26. Duncan S. Ferguson, *Biblical Hermeneutics: An Introduction* (Atlanta: John Knox Press, 1986), 97; Mickelsen, *Interpreting the Bible*, 295-99.

27. Apocalyptic literature is different from prophetic literature. Daniel and Revelation are examples of apocalyptic literature in the Protestant Bible. I agree with Dave Aune that the book of Revelation is a blend of apocalyptic and prophetic literature. Certainly the author intended his book to be prophecy (see Revelation 1:3; 22:7).

28. Ferguson, *Biblical Hermeneutics*, 96.

29. W. Randolph Tate, *Biblical Interpretation: An Integrated Approach* (Peabody: Hendrickson, 1991), 98.

30. Robert Alter, *The Art of Biblical Poetry* (New York: Basic Books, 1985), 11.

31. Tate, *Biblical Interpretation*, 100.

32. David Aune, *The New Testament in its Literary Form* (Philadelphia: Westminster Press, 1987), 183.

33. Ibid., 184-87.

34. Ibid., 188-97.

35. Robert M. Grant and David Tracy, *A Short History on the Interpretation of the Bible* (Philadelphia: Fortress Press, 1984), 3.

36. Bilezikian, *Christianity 101*.

37. Mickelsen, *Interpreting the Bible*, 86-89.

Chapter 5

1. David Buttrick, *Homiletic: Moves and Structures* (Philadelphia: Fortress, 1987), 408.

2. Clyde Fant, *Preaching for Today* (New York: Harper & Row, 1976), 29-30.

3. Craig A. Loscalzo, *Preaching Sermons that Connect* (Downers Grove: InterVarsity Press, 1992).

4. Elizabeth Achtemeier, *Creative Preaching: Finding the Words* (Nashville: Abingdon, 1980), 18.

5. Newbigin, *Foolishness to the Greeks*, 4-5.

6. Henry H. Mitchell, *Celebration and Experience in Preaching* (Nashville: Abingdon, 1991), 68.

7. "Changing Channels: The Wasteland Was Vast in '61" and "What Does Minow Think Now," *Chicago Tribune*, 8 May 1994, sec. 7, 3.

8. Ibid.

9. "The Brain Drain: What Television Is Doing to Us," *Chicago Tribune*, 2 May 1994, sec. 1, 15.

10. See Neil Postman, *Amusing Ourselves to Death! Public Discourse in the Age of Show Business* (New York: Viking Penguin, 1986).

11. Buttrick, *Homiletic*, 408.

12. Long, *Preaching the Literary Forms of the Bible*, 43.

13. Gavin Reid, *The Gagging of God: The Failure of the Church to Communicate in the Television Age* (London: Hodder & Stoughton, 1969), 66-67.

14. Newbigin, *Foolishness to the Greeks*, 4-5.

15. Leander E. Keck, *The Bible in the Pulpit* (Nashville: Abingdon Press, 1978), 101.

16. Ibid., 103-6.

17. Achtemeier, *Creative Preaching: Finding the Words*, 46.

18. Mitchell, *Celebration and Experience in Preaching*, 62.

19. Ibid., 63.

20. Greidanus, *The Modern Preacher and the Ancient Text*, 157.

21. My thanks to friend and colleague Charles H. Cosgrove for this hermeneutical observation.

22. Don M. Wardlaw, ed., *Preaching Biblically: Creating Sermons in the Shape of Scripture* (Philadelphia: Westminster Press, 1983), 68.

23. Cheryl Jarvis, "Look Who's Talking," *Chicago Tribune Magazine* (20 March 1994), 16.

24. Ibid., 14.

25. Ibid., 16.

26. Ibid.

27. Achtemeier, *Creative Preaching*, 104.

28. O. C. Edwards, *Elements of Homiletic: A Method for Preparing to Preach* (New York: Pueblo Publishing Co., 1982), 11.

29. Steven C. Van Ostran, "Showing Ourselves Approved: A Study in Sermon Preparation and Methodology for the Medium-Sized Pastorate" (D.Min. thesis, Northern Baptist Theological Seminary, 1994), 25-37.

30. Haddon W. Robinson, *Biblical Preaching* (Grand Rapids: Baker Book House, 1980), 164.

Chapter 6

1. *Dynamic Communication Workbook* (Arvada, Colo.: Dynamic Communications International, 1990), privately published, 5.

2. James Daane, *Preaching with Confidence: A Theological Essay on the Power of the Pulpit* (Grand Rapids: William B. Eerdmans, 1980), 59.

3. Robinson, *Biblical Preaching*, 32.

4. Gerhard A. Hauser, *Introduction to Rhetorical Theory* (Prospect Heights, Ill.: Waveland Press, 1991), 162-64, 174.

5. Mitchell, *Celebration and Experience in Preaching*, 21.

6. Hauser, *Introduction to Rhetorical Theory*, 65.

7. Fred B. Craddock, *Preaching* (Nashville: Abingdon Press, 1985), 172-74.

8. Wardlaw, ed., *Preaching Biblically*, 16.

9. Buttrick, *Homiletic*, 26.

10. Reuel L. Howe, *Partners in Preaching: Clergy and Laity in Dialogue* (New York: Seabury Press, 1967), 26-33.

11. Buttrick, *Homiletic*, 375.

12. Massey, *Designing the Sermon*, 25.

13. Hauser, *Introduction to Rhetorical Theory*, 88.

14. Ibid., 37, 66, 161.

15. Jeff Scott Cook, *The Element of Speech Writing and Public Speaking* (New York: Macmillan, 1989), 42.

16. Hauser, *Introduction to Rhetorical Theory*, 62-63.

17. Buttrick, *Homiletic*, 388.

18. John M. Ellison, *They Who Preach* (Nashville: Broadman Press, 1956), 66.

19. J. Daniel Baumann, *An Introduction to Contemporary Preaching* (Grand Rapids: Baker Book House, 1972), 79.

20. Michael J. Hostetler, *Introducing the Sermon: The Art of Compelling Beginnings* (Grand Rapids: Zondervan, 1986), 13.

21. Robinson, *Biblical Preaching*, 159.

22. Ibid.

23. Baumann, *An Introduction to Contemporary Preaching*, 136.

24. Hostetler, *Introducing the Sermon*, 13.

25. J. Alfred Smith, *Preach On!* (Nashville: Broadman Press, 1984), 45-46.

26. Mitchell, *Celebration and Experience in Preaching*, 139.

Chapter 7

1. Cook, *The Elements of Speech Writing and Public Speaking*, 154.

2. Arthur Lessac, *The Use and Training of the Human Voice* (New York: Drama Book Specialist, 1967), 3.

3. Uta Hagen, *Respect for Acting* (New York: Macmillan, 1973), 46-51.

4. Ibid., 29.

5. Aristotle, *Rhetoric*. Great Books (Chicago: Encyclopedia Britannica, 1984), vol. 2, 595.

6. Phillips Brooks, *Lectures on Preaching* (New York: E. P. Dutton, 1902), 5-8.

7. Myron R. Chartier, *Preaching as Communication: An Interpersonal Perspective* (Nashville: Abingdon, 1981), 27.

8. Hagen, *Respect for Acting*, 11; Buttrick, *Homeletic*, 11.

9. Richard F. Ward, *Speaking from the Heart: Preaching with Passion* (Nashville: Abingdon, 1992), 27, 55.

10. Chartier, *Preaching as Communication*, 99-111.

Chapter 8

1. "Hello, Carol! Dolly Is Ageless, and so Is Its Star," *Chicago Tribune*, 12 August 1994, sec. 5, 1,5.

2. Pamela A. Moeller, *A Kinesthetic Homiletic: Embodying Gospel in Preaching* (Minneapolis: Augsburg-Fortress, 1993), 4.

3. Steven A. Beebe and Susan J. Beebe, *Public Speaking: An*

Audience-Centered Approach (Englewood Cliffs, N.J.: Prentice Hall, 1991), 223.

4. Ibid., 222-4.

5. Buttrick, *Homiletic*, 69-77; Don M. Wardlaw, ed., *Learning Preaching: Understanding and Participating in the Process* (Lincoln, Ill.: The Lincoln Christian College and Seminary Press, The Academy of Homiletics, 1989), 37-52, 155-200.

6. Moeller, *A Kinesthetic Homiletic*, 16.

7. Richard Boleslavsky, *Acting: The First Six Lessons* (New York: Theatre Arts Books, 1994), 241.

8. Ibid., 3.

9. Jeffrey Hahner, Martin Sokoloff, and Sandra Salisch, *Speaking Clearly: Improving Voice and Diction* (New York: McGraw-Hill, 1990), 11-12.

10. Hahner, et al., *Speaking Clearly*, 11-23; Charles L. Bartow, *The Preaching Moment: A Guide to Sermon Delivery* (Nashville: Abingdon), 69-89; Lessac, *The Use and Training of the Human Voice*, 9-16.

11. Paul Eckman, *Telling Lies: Clues to Deceit in the Marketplace, Politics, and Marriage* (New York: W. W. Norton, 1985), 93-94.

12. Ibid., 286.

13. Cook, *The Elements of Speech Writing and Public Speaking*, 168.

14. Hahner, et al., *Speaking Clearly*, 384.

15. Cook, *The Elements of Speech Writing and Public Speaking*, 168.

16. Beebe and Beebe, *Public Speaking*, 238.

17. Ibid; Cook, *The Elements of Speech Writing and Public Speaking*, 168.

18. Lessac, *The Use and Training of the Human Voice*, 9, 16.

19. Roger E. Axtell, *Do's and Taboos of Public Speaking* (New York: John Wiley, 1992), 65.

20. Bartow, *The Preaching Moment*, 97; Beebe and Beebe, *Speaking Clearly*, 235.

21. Nancy M. Henley, *Body Politics* (New York: Simon and Schuster, 1977), 152.

22. Chartier, *Preaching as Communication*, 83-84.

23. Patricia Webbink, *The Power of the Eyes* (New York: Springer, 1986), 15.

24. Chartier, *Preaching As Communication*, 83-84; Axtell, *Do's and Taboos of Public Speaking*, 65.

25. Bartow, *The Preaching Moment*, 233; Beebe and Beebe, *Public Speaking*, 228-239.

26. Henley, *Body Politics*, 153.

27. Cook, *The Elements of Speech Writing and Public Speaking*, 158.

Chapter 9

1. Paul Galloway, "Three Views Find Science Needs Spiritual Side," *Chicago Tribune*, 31 March 1995, sec. 2, 9.

2. Ronald Allen, "Preaching the Christian Year," in *Handbook of Contemporary Preaching*, ed. Michael Duduit (Nashville: Broadman Press, 1992), 236-244; William D. Thompson, *Preaching Biblically* (Nashville: Abingdon, 1981), 19; Robert Webber, "Preaching through the Lectionary," in *The Renewal of Sunday Worship*, vol. 3 of *The Complete Library of Christian Worship*, ed. Robert Webber (Nashville: Star Song Publishing Group, 1993), 329-330.

3. James W. Cox, *A Guide to Biblical Preaching* (Nashville: Abingdon, 1976), 41.

4. Gardner C. Taylor, *How Shall They Preach?* (Elgin, Ill.: Progressive Baptist Publishing House, 1977), 58.

5. Craig Skinner, "Creativity in Preaching," in *Handbook of Contemporary Preaching*, ed. Michael Duduit (Nashville: Broadman Press, 1992), 562-570; John A. Broadus, *On the Preparation and Delivery of Sermons*, ed. Jesse B. Weatherspoon (New York: Harper & Row, 1944), 281; J. Randall Nichols, *Building the Word: The Dynamics of Communicating and Preaching* (San Francisco: Harper & Row, 1980), 34; Jim Somerville, "Preaching to the Right Brain," *Preaching* 10 (January-February 1995): 36-39; John Sykes, "Preaching to the Left Brain," *Preaching* 10 (January-February 1995): 40-43.

6. Skinner, "Creativity in Preaching," 565.

7. Van Ostran, "Showing Ourselves Approved," 66.